ABSTRACT EXPRESSION

by

Theresa Rebeck

SAMUEL FRENCH, INC.

45 West 25th Street
NEW YORK 10010
LONDON

7623 Sunset Boulevard
HOLLYWOOD 90046
TORONTO

IMPORTANT
BILLING AND CREDIT REQUIREMENTS

All producers of ABSTRACT EXPRESSION *must* give credit to the Author of the Play in all programs distributed in connection with performances of the Play and in all instances in which the title of the Play appears for purposes of advertising, publicizing or otherwise exploiting the Play and/or a production. The name of the Author of the Play *must* appear on a separate line on which no other name appears, immediately following the title, and *must* appear in size of type not less than fifty percent the size of the title type.

All licensees shall be required to give the following acknowledgment on the title page of all programs distributed in connection with the performance of the play:

World Premiere Production presented at The Long Wharf Theatre
Douglas Hughes, Artistic Director   Michael Ross, Executive Director
November 13, 1998

ABSTRACT EXPRESSON was originally produced at Long Wharf Theatre on November 13, 1998. It was directed by Greg Leaming and had the following cast:

Charlie	David Wolos-Fonteno Syl-
Sylvia	Beth Dixon
Lillian	Kristine Nielsen
Eugene	Bray Poor
Lucas/Ray	Larry Gilliard, Jr.
Phillip/Jordy	Glenn Fleshler
Jenny	Angie Phillips
Kidman	Jack Willis
Willie	Mark Nelson

Scenic Design by Neil Patel
Costume Design by David Zinn
Lighting Design by Dan Kotlowitz
Original Music by Fabian Obispo
Sound Design by Matthew Mezick
Wigs by Paul Huntley
Production Stage Manger Kevin E. Thompson

Artistic Director Doug Hughes

CHARACTERS

CHARLIE – Black, mid-fifties
SYLVIA – White, early sixties
LILLIAN – White, late thirties
EUGENE – White, forty
JENNY – White, twenty-eight
KIDMAN – White, early fifties
RAY/LUCAS – Black, late twenties
PHILLIP/JORDY – White, late twenties
WILLIE – White, thirty

SET

The locations vary between Charlie's apartment, quite small and meager, on the lower east side; Sylvia's elegant apartment on the upper east side; the kitchen of Kidman's artist's loft; and the office of Lillian's gallery.

ACT I

Scene 1

(Lights up on a man at a table. He is unloading a bag of groceries and talking to a small bird in a cage on top of a very small television set.)

CHARLIE. Who needs money? Long as we can eat and watch a little television now and then we be okay, hey sweet pea. Look at this, dollar ninety nine for toilet paper, you believe that? Plus they raised the coffee again, I don't really care long as I don't have to drink that stuff tastes like nuts and berries. Four-ninety nine a can. That's a crime. If I was making the rules, I'd keep down the coffee, that's what I say. Only sure way to stave off the revolution. Yeah, don't look at me like that, I got your peanut butter. *(He pulls it out of the bag and looks at it.)* Reduced fat. They charge the same and take things out, that's the way the world, huh. Everything just shrinking down, well, we don't mind. You and me and a good cup of coffee, little television, who needs money. Like a kingdom in here. *(He looks at his mail and stops at a letter. Considers it, then goes back to the can of coffee.)* Make me some coffee.

(He studies the can.
Blackout)

Scene 2

(Lights up on a dinner party. EUGENE, SYLVIA, LILLIAN,
LUCAS and PHILIP are finishing their desert and coffee.)

SYLVIA. I just think the whole thing is much ado about
nothing. I mean, the city has been going to hell as long as I can
remember, I just think it should go there in style and I'm not going to apologize about that.

EUGENE. Don't be ridiculous, Mother.

SYLVIA. I'm not being ridiculous, it's absolutely everywhere in the news again. The gaps between the rich and poor, as
if this were a noteworthy situation, or an actual social condition
or something. When it's really nothing more than a definition. I
mean, it's just what the words mean, isn't it? Some people are
rich, and some are poor, and the poor ones don't have as much
money. How is this news? This is some idiot's idea of news.

LILLIAN. Sylvia. You're just trying to be controversial.

SYLVIA. But I'm not! This isn't even original, what I'm
saying. I mean god, people have been—who was it who said that
thing about poor people being around all the time—

PHILLIP. The poor will be with you always?

EUGENE. That was Jesus Christ, actually.

SYLVIA. There, that's what I mean. Even he was saying it
and he liked them.

(JENNY enters and starts clearing plates.)

LUCAS. Your point being what, Sylvia? I mean, I'm not

saying I disagree with you, but this is starting to make me uncomfortable. I am a person of color after all—

SYLVIA. Oh don't start that. That's not what I'm talking about and you know it. I'm just saying how bad is it really, being poor? Don't you think they're exaggerating, at least a little, the source of all our social problems et cetera, et cetera, well I know plenty of rich people who have social problems. And if the rich are as bad as the poor, socially I mean, or any other way for that matter, well. Then all this fuss is really over nothing.

EUGENE. All what fuss? I don't even know what you're talking about.

SYLVIA. You do too, and don't use that tone with me, young man.

EUGENE. I'm not using a tone, Mother, you're just rattling on about nothing as usual—

SYLVIA. *(Overlap)* Oh really, and may I say your manners are lovely, at your own engagement party which I am paying for I might add—

EUGENE. Oh for god's sake—

SYLVIA. Well, honestly, you're turning into one of those people who hate their own money and I don't have anyone else to leave it to—

EUGENE. Mother—

LILLIAN. Eugene does not hate money. I won't let him.

(She kisses his hand.)

EUGENE. *(Good natured)* Of course I don't hate money, that's ridiculous. I'm just uncomfortable with the assumption that just because you have it that means you know something about social conditions.

PHILLIP. Well why shouldn't it mean that?

EUGENE. When in fact I happen to know that she personally has never spoken to anyone whose trust fund is smaller than two mil on a good day in the market.

SYLVIA. Oh that's not real money—

LILLIAN. *(Laughing)* Sylvia—

EUGENE. *(Animated)* Meanwhile we live in a city where people are starving, literally starving, if the newspapers are to be trusted at all—

PHILLIP. Which they're not—

SYLVIA. Oh, nobody starves on Manhattan. Manhattan is thirty-four square miles of room service, my father used to say that.

(They all laugh.)

EUGENE. Not that I care, I don't care. I just don't know why you keep going on about it.

SYLVIA. Oh, now you're upset.

EUGENE. I'm not upset.

LILLIAN. What about you, are you poor?

(She looks at JENNY. JENNY stops her cleaning for a moment and looks up, surprised.)

PHILLIP. *(Amused)* Oh really, Lillian.

LILLIAN. What's it like?

EUGENE. Lillian.

SYLVIA. Oh no, that's not what I meant at all. I don't want

to know what it's like, that's not the point.
     LUCAS. No, I think it is.

(JENNY starts for the door, carrying plates.)

     LILLIAN. Where are you going? I asked you a question.
     JENNY. *(Surprised)* Oh.
     LUCAS. You're serious.

     LILLIAN. Eugene has a point. I don't see how we can talk about this, consider ourselves informed on any level, if we're not willing to confront the reality of poverty in the city. *(To JENNY)* So what's it like? Can you tell us?

     SYLVIA. Yes but she's not poor. Look at her, she's clearly educated. You're educated, aren't you, you're an actress or something.

     LUCAS. Actresses are poor.
     JENNY. I'm not an actress.
     SYLVIA. But you're educated.

(There is an awkward pause at this.)

     JENNY. I've been to high school.
     SYLVIA. Not college?
     JENNY. No.
     LILLIAN. But you graduated high school.
     JENNY. *(A slight beat)* I haven't, actually. Excuse me.

(She heads for the door, with the plates.)

     SYLVIA. Oh, you dropped out, is that it? To be an actress,

or something?

EUGENE. She already said she's not an actress, mother. *(To JENNY)* I'm sorry. You need to finish up, and we're keeping you.

SYLVIA. All of a sudden you're so sensitive, well, she can just answer the question before she goes. What is it like to be poor?

(They stare at JENNY. She considers this.)

JENNY. It's like not having enough money.

SYLVIA. This is my point...

JENNY. You worry a lot.

SYLVIA. You worry? Well I worry.

EUGENE. You worry about your nails, and whether or not you can get theatre tickets.

JENNY. Did you need anything else?

LILLIAN. Stop trying to run off, this is interesting.

JENNY. It's not interesting. It's not. It's just, you don't have enough money. That's all it is. You skip breakfast. You buy cheap shoes. You stand in the drug store and try to figure out how much it costs per aspirin if you buy the big bottle instead of the little one, and all you can think is of course it's better to just spend the money and have the big bottle because then you've paid less per aspirin, but if you do that, there won't be enough left to go to a movie and sometimes you just want to go to a movie. You'd be amazed at how long you can think about that. Then you think about other cities where movies don't cost ten dollars and you get mad, 'cause ten dollars is a lot, for a movie, it's... It's boring, really. A lot of boring things stick in your head for a long time. You just, you think about money all the time.

EUGENE. *(Dry)* So in one way at least, it is like being rich.

SYLVIA. Don't your parents help you?

JENNY. My mother's dead.

PHILLIP. What about your father, doesn't he work?

JENNY. No, he does work, he works very hard. But he's, actually, he's an artist.

LILLIAN. An artist? You mean a painter?

JENNY. Yes.

SYLVIA. Oh, that's different. Her father's an artist. So she's poor, but it doesn't count.

EUGENE. Why not?

SYLVIA. Artists are supposed to be poor. It helps their art. And don't argue with me about this, I'm right about this.

LILLIAN. *(Interested)* What's his name?

JENNY. Walter Kidman.

LILLIAN. Mac Kidman?

(There is a surprised stir at this. JENNY is clearly startled.)

LUCAS. *(Amused)* My god, Lillian. You know this man?

LILLIAN. Is it him?

JENNY. *(Now truly uncomfortable)* Yes, actually.

LILLIAN. No one's heard from him in years. He's still painting?

JENNY. Of course he's still painting. That's what he is, he's a painter.

PHILLIP. *(To LILLIAN)* Is he any good?

LILLIAN. There was some debate about it, but he had something of a career, what, fifteen or twenty years ago. My uncle reviewed one of his shows. He didn't much like that particular batch, but he always felt he had talent.

JENNY. Your uncle?

LILLIAN. Yes, he was the art critic for *The Times*. You must've been a child, I'm sure you don't remember.

JENNY. Of course I remember. It was his last show.

LILLIAN. Was it?

JENNY. I have to go.

(She suddenly turns and heads for the door.)

LILLIAN. *(Calling)* But your father's still painting?

JENNY. *(Tense)* Yes. He is.

LILLIAN. I'd love to see what he's doing these days. I have a gallery. Lillian Paul. My uncle had terrific respect for your father. He just thought he was going down the wrong track, I think.

(A beat. JENNY doesn't respond. She finally turns and goes.)

SYLVIA. Well, that was rude.

EUGENE. For god's sake. You were examining her like she was some kind of bug!

SYLVIA. We were expressing interest. How is that a bad thing?

PHILLIP. This Kidman was good, you say?

LILLIAN. Not likely but for god's sake you can't say that to the man's daughter. What kind of a bitch do you think I am?

(They laugh.
Blackout)

Scene 3

(Kidman's loft. KIDMAN and CHARLIE sit at a table, getting drunk on Jack Daniels. They are looking at a painting.)

CHARLIE. I like it.

(KIDMAN goes to the painting and turns it so that it now stands horizontal, which is the correct way to look at it.)

KIDMAN. It's shit.

CHARLIE. No, it's good.

KIDMAN. No, I mean, yeah, it's good shit. But Jesus, this bullshit—

CHARLIE. That part, looks like a duck?

KIDMAN. What?

CHARLIE. It looks like a little duck in a lake, or one of those birds with the legs. And the things over there...

KIDMAN. What things?

CHARLIE. You know, those things grow out of the water. Bulrushes.

KIDMAN. *(Annoyed)* Those aren't—this is not a duck, all right?

CHARLIE. Then what is it?

KIDMAN. It's abstract. It's not anything.

CHARLIE. If it's not anything, it can be a duck.

KIDMAN. No it can't.

CHARLIE. That's what you said before. Before, you said—

KIDMAN. It's abstract.

CHARLIE. So, it's an abstract duck.

KIDMAN. It's nonrepresentational!

CHARLIE. *(Overlap)* I'm just pulling your leg. You get all worked up and start using words, I'm just having a conversation here. Good lord.

KIDMAN. *(Overlap)* I'm having a conversation. Am I not having a conversation? I'm just saying it's not a duck.

CHARLIE. Yeah, okay...

KIDMAN. This line is shit. Look at this, it's like some giant worm.

(He looks for a brush.)

CHARLIE. Leave it alone, I like it.

KIDMAN. You think it looks like a duck! I mean Jesus, you're like some fucking German expressionist, why don't I just put a woman and a tree in there, that would really make it good—

CHARLIE. Oh cut it out.

KIDMAN. Those idiot Germans acting like they invented the moon, when they didn't even— *(He starts to smudge something.)* Fucking philosophical shitheads. Look at this. Aw shit.

CHARLIE. Leave it alone!

KIDMAN. Hey, who's the painter, you or me?

CHARLIE. I'm just saying—

KIDMAN. Who's the painter?

CHARLIE. Don't pull that shit on me. You want to fuck that up, be my guest, but all I'm saying you should calm down, stop being such an asshole and just accept the fact, that's a damn duck.

(KIDMAN sits and stares at it.)

KIDMAN. Fuck, I'm fucked. It's a fucking duck.

(He laughs. CHARLIE laughs, too. KIDMAN pours another round of drinks and stands to put the painting away.)

CHARLIE. Well, I like it.

KIDMAN. You want it?

CHARLIE. You mean to have? You throwing that away?

KIDMAN. I'm not throwing it away. I'm giving it to you.

CHARLIE. Don't you throw that away. That's good, I'm telling you.

KIDMAN. I'm not throwing it away, I'm giving it to you.

CHARLIE. 'Cause a lot of people might like a picture like that.

KIDMAN. You don't want it?

CHARLIE. I didn't say that. I been saying I like it.

KIDMAN. But you don't want it.

CHARLIE. I'm just saying you could sell that for a lot of money.

KIDMAN. What are you, nuts?

CHARLIE. They sell pictures, people make a lot of money off pictures like this.

KIDMAN. Really? No, really?

CHARLIE. Yeah I know you being smart with me. All I'm saying, one day, we'll be singing and dancing 'cause you gonna be rich.

KIDMAN. 'Cause the market for paintings of ducks is about to take off.

CHARLIE. That's what I said.

KIDMAN. Too bad it's not painted on velvet, that would make it really good.

(They laugh. JENNY enters, still in her catering outfit, carrying a large paper bag of leftover food.)

JENNY. Hey Charlie. Hi, Daddy.

(CHARLIE whisks the bottle off the table and holds it between his legs on the floor. Happily involved in her own news, JENNY doesn't notice it at first.)

CHARLIE. Hey, honey.

KIDMAN. Hey, where'd you go? I turned around and you were gone.

JENNY. I took this catering gig at the last minute, I so did not want to do it but they were begging, and I thought, well maybe I can work this into a favor from Bernie sometime, so I went and I was the only one working, right, and these people are kind of a nightmare but they could not care less about the leftovers, which is like, I mean, excuse me. Chicken with mustard tarragon sauce.

CHARLIE. Oh my goodness, how 'bout that.

JENNY. Stuffed acorn squash.

KIDMAN. Oh, this is fantastic.

JENNY. Creme brulee. I love even just saying that, creme brulee. Creme brulee. I got all of it, most of these people are, they're all so worried about getting fat they've completely forgotten how to eat. Creme bru—

*(She sees the bottle of whiskey on the floor. The mood changes.
CHARLIE looks embarrassed. KIDMAN becomes immediately defiant, openly picking up the bottle. He takes a mug
full of paint brushes off the table, knocks the brushes out and
makes a show of pouring a large drink.)*

CHARLIE. I guess we gonna have a feast, huh? *(Beat)* Just come up to watch the game. My TV busted.

JENNY. *(Still trying to recover)* Oh, huh?

CHARLIE. *(Tap dancing now)* Picture don't even come in, just scramble, you know. So I come up here, saying I'll just watch on your set, then Mac, he can't even find it. Put it away somewhere, he don't even know.

KIDMAN. It's here somewhere.

JENNY. So you couldn't find the TV, so you decided to get trashed.

(A beat. CHARLIE is embarrassed. KIDMAN is not.)

CHARLIE. Oh now.

KIDMAN. That's right, we took your hard-earned money and said what's the surest way to piss that girl off? What's gonna really tie her up? How can I make my long-suffering daughter suffer even more?

JENNY. Daddy. You promised.

KIDMAN. "Daddy, you promised."

JENNY. *(Patient)* Yes, you promised, and I don't know why you'd, it's been months, and everything's fine, you were doing, we're—

KIDMAN. Oh now I have to justify myself to my daughter?

Is that where we're at? I'm such a sorry hack I have to lie to everybody when I want a drink or you're what, you're gonna cut off my allowance—

JENNY. You told me—

CHARLIE. We was just having one drink, Jenny.

JENNY. Charlie, half the damn bottle is—I'm not—no.

(She dumps the food and heads for the next room, trying not to lose it.)

KIDMAN. *(Yelling after her)* You're an old woman!

JENNY. You're a drunk!

KIDMAN. Oh you really cut me. That's a hit. Oh my—

JENNY. I can't believe this. I've been working like an animal, serving eight courses to assholes so we can pay for some heat in this—I can't even—I'm begging scraps of food and you're back here killing yourself! You know that stuff will kill you, and—

KIDMAN. Christ you need to get laid.

JENNY. *(Losing it)* I WOULD get laid if I had a life instead of— *(Beat)* I'm such an idiot. I'm just a complete fucking idiot.

KIDMAN. That's my girl.

JENNY. Fuck you.

KIDMAN. Yeah, fuck you too.

CHARLIE. No, now, Jenny! You know, we was just having a nip. *(There is a terrible pause while KIDMAN glares at her. She doesn't know what to do. She sits, finally. KIDMAN prowls. CHARLIE looks at them both, nervous. Continuing; tap dancing again)* Did I tell you? Got a letter from my sister's boy, Ray. He's finally gettin' out of the joint. I say that's a good thing, you know, but he been in there upwards four years, so who knows. Wants to come stay with me, I'm thinking, well, I don't know about that. Ain't exactly a palace down there. Don't have the kind of room you all got. Plus the TV's on the blink. Well I told you that.

(He stops, unhappy, wondering what the others will do. JENNY wipes her eyes and finally looks up, resigned.)

JENNY. Ray? Did I meet him once?

CHARLIE. Well maybe you did. You remember that, you got a good head on your shoulders, cause that would be a long time ago. 'Course you got a good head, we know that. *(JENNY sobs, briefly.)* Oh now honey. You're okay.

(KIDMAN prowls, restless.)

KIDMAN. I don't ask for this. You want to take off, take off. No one's begging you to prostrate yourself on the altar of filial devotion. Your brother had the balls to leave. You want a life, go get one.

JENNY. I'm going to bed.

KIDMAN. Just don't come home expecting people to genuflect, you're so holy, you're so good. Your life is your own.

CHARLIE. You're going to bed? I thought we was gonna have a party. All this nice food.

JENNY. You eat it.

CHARLIE. Oh now Jenny.

JENNY. I just don't know why I even—these people were hideous, they—and you think that's nothing? That I have to stand there and take it, the whole time I'm just thinking, pay me. I'm doing the job, why can't you just pay me, you sons of bitches, why do I have to be humiliated to just get the damn MONEY. *(Beat)* Fuck it. *(She heads for her room, speaking as she goes.)* Oh. By the way. One of them knew who you were. Her uncle was that critic who said your sense of color was pre-adolescent.

KIDMAN. Asshole.

JENNY. She wants to see your work. She has a gallery, Lillian something.

KIDMAN. You didn't even get her damn name?

JENNY. Lillian Paul, all right—

KIDMAN. Yeah, Lillian Paul, and I'm supposed to jump, is that it? They're coming crawling now, I'm supposed to go pay obeisance to some cunt wouldn't know a real painting unless she pissed on it—

JENNY. Never mind.

KIDMAN. Did you tell her she can go fuck herself? Did you tell her that?

(There is a short beat while JENNY looks at her father.)

JENNY. No. I didn't.

(Blackout)

Scene 4

(It is the middle of the night. KIDMAN sits at the table, totally drunk, surrounded by half-open boxes of leftovers and the now near-empty bottle of Jack. JENNY enters, in a t-shirt and old pajama bottoms. She looks at him, in the half-light.)

JENNY. It's three in the morning. You should go to bed.
KIDMAN. All this food. I was gonna...
JENNY. Just go to bed.

(She starts to put away the food.)

KIDMAN. That stuff is shit. It's shit anyway. I was in Pisa, with your mother, we had creme brulee, that was the real stuff. Got in a fight with some asshole on the street, he's screaming at me in Italian, right? I did something, who knows, your mom gets so embarrassed, she starts screaming back at him in German. He's yelling Privato! Privato! And your mom is, she was embarrassed, so she starts talking German, so this guy doesn't know we're American idiots. Ich ben Deutch something, wasser bitte, shit like this.

JENNY. And then you had creme brulee.

KIDMAN. She did. I ordered ... pear tart with avocado sauce. She hated pears. Only ever had two in her life, that she liked. One was in France. The other... Spent years, trying to get her to eat another pear. Big thing with her. The search for pear number three. *(Beat)* You got that from her. This thing for food. The woman would take a bite of something and swoon. Thought a corn dog was a gift from god.

JENNY. Well. Corn dogs.

KIDMAN. She was like that. Skinny as a twig. Loved food. Any food. Except pears.

(Beat)

JENNY. How was it?

KIDMAN. Huh?

JENNY. The pear tart with avocado sauce.

KIDMAN. It was Italy. Pear number three.

JENNY. *(After a beat)* You should go to bed.

KIDMAN. I was gonna paint. You went to bed and I was, but I can't...

JENNY. It'll be okay tomorrow.

KIDMAN. *(An apology)* This is—I didn't—It's just, the painting is shit right now—

JENNY. It's not, Daddy.

KIDMAN. You don't know.

JENNY. I do know. There's no light now. You can't, you're drunk, and—

KIDMAN. Don't you fucking throw that at me—

JENNY. Daddy, there's no light! It's three in the morning. There's no light.

(The force of this argument actually gets through to him. He nods.)

KIDMAN. That fucking prick. Preadolescent.

JENNY. *(Patient)* He was an asshole.

KIDMAN. Dead now, you know. That's the only good thing you can say about critics. Eventually, they're gonna die, just like everyone else. They come up with these words, preadolescent, it's primitive, we're doing something, but ever since Picasso, you can't use that word as an insult so they come up with something else because they don't want to spend half a brain cell thinking what someone's trying to do.

JENNY. Daddy, your paintings are beautiful. It doesn't matter what he said.

KIDMAN. That's what I'm saying.

JENNY. They didn't stop you. You still did it. And they're beautiful.

KIDMAN. They tried to stop me.

JENNY. They lost.

(Beat)

KIDMAN. I'm murdering you.

JENNY. No.

KIDMAN. There's such light in you.

JENNY. There's light in you, Daddy. There's light in you.

(He cannot look at her.
Blackout)

Scene 5

(The office of Lillian Paul. LILLIAN sits at her desk. CHARLIE stands before her, holding a painting.)

LILLIAN. Where did you get this?

CHARLIE. My friend give it to me. Walter Kidman, he's a friend of mine.

LILLIAN. Really.

CHARLIE. See I know him and his girl Jenny, who said she met you and you said, you wanted to see what kind of painting Walter was making, 'cause you remembered him from before.

LILLIAN. And he sent you as his emissary.

CHARLIE. He don't know I'm here.

LILLIAN. Such a surprise.

CHARLIE. 'Scuse me?

LILLIAN. No, continue.

CHARLIE. Well, he's a little contentious on account that's just how he is, but he give me this painting, and when Jenny said you remembered Walter I thought maybe I could sell it.

LILLIAN. This is yours to sell?

CHARLIE. Yeah, he give it to me. It's a present.

LILLIAN. He gave you a present, and now you're selling it? That's not very nice.

CHARLIE. Well, I'm way out of cash, and that's a fact. My nephew's coming to stay with me, my TV's busted, and now they's these cuts the goverment keeps talking about. I don't know. Spent two years in Viet Nam, that don't seem to mean much to people, but can't change the world, I guess.

LILLIAN. I guess not.

(She looks at the painting. CHARLIE watches her, nervous.)

CHARLIE. 'Cause see, I really like it. Don't get me wrong about that. That's how come I'm here, Jenny said you expressed interest, and I thought, she don't even know, on account nobody's been seeing what all Walter can do for how long. This is a fine piece of work. I think it looks like a duck. *(A beat, then, as she doesn't respond)* 'Cause you can see him, swimming on the lake, with those things, look like bulrushes to me. I know, you're not supposed to do that. Decide what it looks like.

LILLIAN. Why not?

CHARLIE. I don't know. Walter, he just gets worked up sometimes, when you suggest stuff like that.

LILLIAN. And how much are you asking?

CHARLIE. 'Scuse me?

LILLIAN. Your price. How much would you like me to pay for it?

(There is a bit of a pause at this, as CHARLIE never quite expected to get this far.)

CHARLIE. Oh, I don't, you know. You'd know more about that. *(She shrugs. He looks about, uncomfortable, then decides to go for it.)* It's art and all, so that's worth something. That's all I'm saying. *(Beat. She waits.)* I was thinking six hundred dollars. Maybe seven, even.

LILLIAN. Which, six or seven?

CHARLIE. Seven.

LILLIAN. Six.
CHARLIE. Whoa, really? Okay. Six.
LILLIAN. Sold.

*(CHARLIE grins, having hit the jackpot, and even laughs a little.
His laugher becomes uncomfortable.*
Blackout)

Scene 6

*(Sylvia's apartment. LILLIAN is laughing. EUGENE is looking at
the painting. SYLVIA bustles about, serving tea.)*

SYLVIA. Well, I just don't know what you're saying.

LILLIAN. I'm saying I bought a painting, a very good painting.

SYLVIA. From that girl's father? That cater-person who told
us what it's like to be poor, and then went on and on—

LILLIAN. *(Overlap)* Oh god, I feel terrible about that. I was
drunk—

SYLVIA. Why do you feel terrible? She was very well-paid.
And she took all the leftovers, I think we treated her very well.

LILLIAN. *(To EUGENE)* Yes, but what do you think?

EUGENE. I...

LILLIAN. You don't like it?

EUGENE. No, I do, I just...

LILLIAN. Because I love it. Look what he's doing with perspective, it's like the whole thing moves, look—

EUGENE. This isn't my forte, Lillian. I mean, you never show this stuff.

SYLVIA. No one's interested in abstract expressionism, because you can never tell if it's any good. That's the problem with it.

LILLIAN. You can tell. This is good.

EUGENE. He actually showed up, then? The father?

LILLIAN. No, god no. This is fabulous. This old black man showed up, dressed like you wouldn't—I mean, I almost called security, this guy looks like he's living on the street, but he's carrying this painting. Turns out they're friends, and he needs cash.

EUGENE. How much did you give him?

LILLIAN. Six hundred dollars.

SYLVIA. For that? No. Really? You paid six hundred dollars for that?

LILLIAN. I'm telling you, Sylvia, I love it. And not only that, I think it's going to be worth something.

(She goes up behind EUGENE and hugs him, enthusiastic. He looks at her, bemused.)

EUGENE. I haven't seen you like this, ever.

LILLIAN. *(Laughing)* I know! I'm just so ... you get so sick of this damn bullshit, putting together group shows, schmoozing the fucking critics, just to get them into an opening once in a while, following who's showing what in some stupid gallery in Minneapolis for god's sake, forcing a sale out of a friend so that you can generate some little bit of heat for someone who's really good, it's all just, nothing is a bit of fun since Black Thursday, when the hell are we going to recover from that, that's what I want to know. And then to have something different happen, something really different. You should have seen this guy. And what did that girl say, this guy's been out there for years, painting, he's been painting for fifteen years in some garret, probably, and not showing anywhere. Abject poverty, blah blah blah—

SYLVIA. *(Interested)* You mean like Van Gogh?

EUGENE. Not Van Gogh again, when are we going to—

LILLIAN. Come on, this is a story, Gene. I can do something with this.

EUGENE. A story. And here I am, thinking you liked the painting.

LILLIAN. I love the painting. The painting is fantastic, that's what makes the story so good. If the painting's no good, the story is just pathetic. But the painting is fantastic.

SYLVIA. How can you know that? It's abstract. Who can tell if those things are any good?

(LILLIAN is now looking for pen and paper.)

LILLIAN. We have to find Kidman. Sylvia, that catering company, what's the phone number. We have to track that girl down.

EUGENE. I already did. *(LILLIAN looks at him, surprised.)* I felt bad. Forgot to give her her tip.

(He hands a card to LILLIAN. She considers this, and him, as SYLVIA speaks.)

SYLVIA. *(Preoccupied, looking at painting)* Don't be ridiculous. I tipped her the way I always do.

EUGENE. Exactly.

SYLVIA. *(Rattling on)* Plus I let her take all that food, she did very well by us. Well, I just don't see it, Lillian. I'm glad you're excited, but I have to say, if I'm going to hang something on the wall, it should look like something. Well, I suppose you could say that's a bird, or a duck over there. I suppose you could say that.

(Blackout)

Scene 7

(Kidman's apartment. EUGENE stands at one side, casually disinterested. JENNY waits, nervous.)

EUGENE. They've been in there for a while.

JENNY. Yes.

EUGENE. She was very enthusiastic. About the one painting. She doesn't get this way. *(Beat)* How many does he have? I mean, I just got a glimpse. Looked like quite a few.

JENNY. Yes.

(She paces.)

EUGENE. Hundreds, even. Fifteen years worth, I guess.

JENNY. Look, why are you here?

EUGENE. She liked his work. It's not unusual for gallery owners. Visiting an artist in his studio, that's—

JENNY. No one has been interested in him for years.

EUGENE. So this is a good thing. Right? Which is why you're so cheerful.

JENNY. I just think you should go. I mean, I didn't say anything, at that dinner party, but, this isn't, you don't know what—

EUGENE. Look. I wanted to apologize about that. The way people spoke to you was inappropriate, and—

JENNY. No. I'm not—

EUGENE. Well, I wanted to apologize.

JENNY. I'm not— *(Beat)* You know, does your girlfriend know you were hitting on me at your own engagement party?

EUGENE. I was what?

JENNY. Oh, you weren't hitting on me. In the kitchen.

EUGENE. No.

JENNY. "What's that perfume you're wearing?"

EUGENE. I wanted to—

JENNY. I wasn't wearing—

EUGENE. So you said. I asked a question, you answered it. That's hardly—

JENNY. "Do you want to go have a drink sometime?" That's not—

EUGENE, It was an honest—

JENNY. *(Starting to laugh)* Oh my god. It was your own engagement party and you were, and now—

EUGENE. Lillian wanted to see your father's paintings, and I came along. I admit I find you interesting. That's not a crime.

JENNY. Interesting? What? I'm what?

EUGENE. Interesting. You seem—

JENNY. Interesting?

EUGENE. Yes. Interesting.

JENNY. *(Matter-of-fact, confrontational)* Don't you mean "pretty?" That I seem pretty?

EUGENE. I mean what I said. You seemed interesting.

JENNY. Then I'm not pretty.

EUGENE. Of course you're pretty. That's not what I was talking about.

JENNY. *(Finally defiant)* So you would find me just as interesting if I weren't pretty? If I were some sort of huge fat person? Or some little nerdy boy with greasy hair and glasses, but the same person, I'd be just as interesting to you?

EUGENE. If you were those things, you wouldn't be the same person.

JENNY. Funny, somehow I knew you were going to say that.

EUGENE. Do you think I'm hitting on you?

JENNY. No. I think you find me "interesting."

EUGENE. *(Growing amusement)* Yes, you grow more interesting by the second.

JENNY. Oh good.

EUGENE. You weren't like this at all the other night. I mean, you're very—

JENNY. *(Frustrated finally)* What?

EUGENE. Nothing. Interesting.

(LILLIAN and KIDMAN reenter the room. KIDMAN and LILLIAN are deep into it. LILLIAN is happily enthralled.)

KIDMAN. Yeah, it's possible he wasn't a complete vegetable, I'm just saying, people admit he didn't even paint—

LILLIAN. Unquestionably, his assistants were doing some of the work. But there's plenty of critical discussion about—

KIDMAN. Don't you fucking talk to me about critical discussion. I'll kick you out of my fucking studio, you—

LILLIAN. But that's not what we're talking about. We're talking about what you think.

KIDMAN. About de Koonig.

LILLIAN. Yes.

KIDMAN. Yeah, see, I don't think that's what we're talking about.

(He looks at her. She gives him a slight nod of acknowledgement.)

LILLIAN. I think that many things inform an artist's work, and many things taint it. Your work is untainted but not uninformed. I would say it's a tragedy that you haven't been showing all these years, but I don't think you could've done this otherwise. The sense of privacy and turbulent isolation, it's absolutely stunning. My future mother-in-law says the problem with abstract expressionism is that no one understands it, but it's impossible to misunderstand the greatness of your paintings. Really, I haven't any words.

EUGENE. And yet.

LILLIAN. *(Excited, oblivious)* Yes, and yet I could go on! But I won't. I'm going to show these paintings, Walter. And I'm not talking about next year; I'm talking about now. Next month. This is absolutely the right time, no one's seen anything like this in years. Fuck de Koonig, we've got Walter Kidman back from

the dead! These paintings make the post post modernists I've
been showing look like pure bullshit—

KIDMAN. They look like that anyway, Lillian.

LILLIAN. *(Laughing)* Oh, Walter. This is going to be fun.

*(She takes his hand and smiles at him. He doesn't quite know
what to make of this.)*

JENNY. Well, that's just—

LILLIAN. What?

JENNY. Crazy. I mean, this is just—crazy.

LILLIAN. I don't think so.

JENNY. Well, but, so are we supposed to clap? No one's
even spoken to him in fifteen years and now we're supposed to
jump up and down because you like his paintings?

KIDMAN. What's your problem?

JENNY. Dad, they're not even—they didn't even come over
here because—oh, shit.

LILLIAN. Oh.

JENNY. I mean its...

KIDMAN. *(Offended)* What? It's what?

JENNY. *(Defiant)* It's crazy.

KIDMAN. Since you know so much about it.

JENNY. Dad.

KIDMAN. I mean, I thought I was the one painting my guts
out for fifteen years. I didn't realize—

JENNY. Oh, for—you're the one who said it! All this time—

KIDMAN. *(Overlap)* You were the great genius behind the
throne.

JENNY. *(Overlap)* You've been doing this for fifteen years

without them!

KIDMAN. Don't you fucking talk to me like an idiot—

JENNY. You're the one who, you keep saying, what do you need them for?

KIDMAN. It's not a question of needing them. I don't need them.

JENNY. Exactly. You did that, before, and they treated you-- You did what she's talking about, the galleries, and the critics, and it almost killed you!

KIDMAN. Oh no no.

LILLIAN. The critical environment is very different now, if you're concerned about—

KIDMAN. We're not concerned.

EUGENE. We should go.

KIDMAN. No. She's nuts. She's got like no life, she's a nun in training, it's made her—

JENNY. No one would take your damn phone calls! Sending slides out into the void, galleries couldn't even be bothered to send a rejection letter! All because one asshole in *The New York Times*—

LILLIAN. It's a little more complicated than—

JENNY. It wasn't more complicated to us. My mother died. We had no health insurance, we had no heat—

KIDMAN. *(Cutting her off)* She had cancer!

LILLIAN. *(Alert)* Your wife died of cancer?

EUGENE. We can come back.

JENNY. Don't. This doesn't have anything to do with you. All those years, you left us alone, and it almost killed him, but then it didn't, and that's what he did. Now all a sudden, you show up, and he's supposed to jump? You can forget it. He doesn't need you. He doesn't need anything you can offer. He doesn't need it.

(There is a silence at this. LILLIAN looks at KIDMAN, who looks down. She nods.)

LILLIAN. All right, look. This was very sudden. I'm a little, I can't say I'm enthusiastic by nature, because I'm not, so maybe I got carried away. Why don't you think about it for a few days.

(She waits a beat, then looks at EUGENE and turns to go.)

KIDMAN. *(To JENNY)* Yeah, we're not thinking about this, 'cause I'm gonna do it. I mean, what are you, insane? Are you completely insane?

(Beat)

LILLIAN. Is there someplace we can go and talk?
KIDMAN. Let's go get a drink. *(To LILLIAN, as he goes)* My friends call me Mac.
LILLIAN. Well, Mac, how about some champagne?

(She laughs and they go, leaving JENNY alone. EUGENE stops for a moment, wanting to say something. She looks at him. Blackout)

Scene 8

(Charlie's apartment. RAY, energetic and edgy, looks around the small room.)

RAY. This is great, Uncle Charlie. Fantastic.

CHARLIE. *(Cautious)* It ain't big or nothin'. I mean, you gonna have to maybe sleep in the couch.

RAY. Kitchen floor do for me. Hey, you got a bird. What's your name, bird?

CHARLIE. That's Swee'pea.

RAY. Swee'pea. That's nice.

CHARLIE. *(Lecturing)* And I know you're gonna work hard and meet your obligations. It's not easy comin' out of the slammer, and I told Charlotte I'd give you a hand, but you gonna have to work. She says that's part of the parole. You want to rest your coat?

RAY. No, I'm okay. And Uncle Charlie, trust me, you don't have to worry 'bout that other stuff, 'cause I am not going back. I'm a reformed person. Look at this, a new TV.

CHARLIE. *(Uncomfortable making small talk)* Yeah, the other one it just finally busted. My friend Mac give me a picture he painted, and I had to sell it for the money. Woman give me six hundred dollars for it.

RAY. Six hundred dollars? For a picture of what?

CHARLIE. It's not that kind of picture.

RAY. What kind of picture is it?

CHARLIE. It kinda looks like a duck.

RAY. Six hundred dollars for a picture of a duck. And

probably she woulda paid a lot more, that's how those things work. White woman, right?

CHARLIE. *(Uncomfortable)* She was white, sure, but she didn't seem like she was taking advantage. I mean, I wouldn't say that.

RAY. That picture was probably worth two or three thousand dollars. You think she gonna pay you what it's worth? I don't think so. Black man comes to her with something she wants, she ain't gonna say let's do the right thing for this black man. She gonna say, how much can I steal this for. 'Cause that's what they like to do. It ain't worth it to them 'less they rob you.

CHARLIE. I don't think that's what it was. 'Cause she give me the whole six hundred. Paid for the whole television out of that. Plus a toaster oven and a microwave.

RAY. If she give you six right out, that's 'cause she don't want you thinking about it! You got that money in your pocket, you ain't thinking about nothin', that's what they like! She don't want you thinkin', how come she's trying to get rid of me so fast? Maybe six hundred isn't such a good deal now. White women, that's how they work. Lookin' to make you a fool, that's how they work.

CHARLIE. Well, I don't know about that.

RAY. You got peanut butter? 'Cause all I'm saying, you got to be aware of what the white man's tryin' to do to you. I spent four years in prison for a robbery I didn't even do, and I regret none of it, you know why? 'Cause it taught me 'bout the world. Now I see what's comin', 'cause of what the white man and the black man mean to each other. There is going to be a racial explosion and that's just a fact. Other than that, the only solution is a complete separation between the black race and the white race.

CHARLIE. Some of them okay, now.

RAY. They's some tarantulas okay too, only I don't want 'em sleepin' in my bed. Look at this place, all you got's four walls and a bird, that white woman won't even let you buy a decent TV. That's all I'm saying. You went to Viet Nam.

(There is a pause at this, as RAY eats peanut butter.)

CHARLIE. *(Finally)* Little more money, I coulda got cable, I guess.

RAY. That's what I'm sayin'. That's all I'm sayin'.

*(He continues eating peanut butter.
Blackout)*

Scene 9

(Sylvia's apartment. Another dinner party is in full swing. This time, KIDMAN is one of the guests. They are looking at a painting.)

SYLVIA. Do you like it?

KIDMAN. Like? I don't know. It's hard to talk about paintings that way.

SYLVIA. How would you talk about it?

KIDMAN. Well, I wouldn't go so far as to say that it's bad.

For instance, it's not that I wouldn't piss on it if it was burning. But that's sort of the general area I'd use in discussing it.

SYLVIA. Oh really.

KIDMAN. It's just not my kind of thing.

PHILLIP. Why don't you like it?

KIDMAN. You mean, besides the fact that it's ugly?

LILLIAN. It's never been my favorite, either, Sylvia—

SYLVIA. What do you mean, you never told me that.

EUGENE. I think—

SYLVIA. You stay out of this. Well I don't care. I like it very much. This artist is very successful.

KIDMAN. Oh yeah, well then what I do I know.

PHILLIP. Not only that, but this particular piece has been especially well-reviewed.

KIDMAN. Oh, the asshole critics like it, there you go. That means it's art.

SYLVIA. No, it's not just that, although they're professionals, I don't see why I shouldn't take their recommendations. I do take their recommendations, and besides that, I like it a great deal.

LILLIAN. That's what matters.

KIDMAN. No it's not. I mean, this is—can I have more of this?

(He holds up his glass. EUGENE refills it.)

SYLVIA. It doesn't matter that I like it?

KIDMAN. No, because you don't know anything.

SYLVIA. Lillian!

LILLIAN. *(Trying to save this)* Maybe we should eat.

(She steers them to the table, where they sit.)

SYLVIA. Well, I don't like abstract paintings. So clearly, there are just different opinions on this matter.

KIDMAN. Yeah. Right ones, and wrong ones.

LUCAS. You've hurt her feelings, she doesn't mean it. You like some abstract paintings, Sylvia. I took you to the de Kooning retrospective, you loved it.

SYLVIA. I was being polite. Oh some of it was all right, I like the colors. I just don't like it when I can't tell what a picture's about.

LILLIAN. It's about whatever you want it to be about. However it makes you feel.

SYLVIA. I know, I know, but I don't like that.

KIDMAN. *(Fed up)* Then don't look at it.

SYLVIA. Well, that's no answer.

KIDMAN. Yes it is.

SYLVIA. Well, I have to look at it. If I don't I won't ever know if I can like it.

KIDMAN. You just said you didn't.

SYLVIA. Maybe I'll change my mind.

KIDMAN. *(Getting fed up with this)* Who cares if you change your mind? You're a moron!

SYLVIA. Oh really!

LILLIAN. *(Again trying to save this)* I think what Mac means is he doesn't particularly feel the need to defend his idiom. Nor should he. It's like a Frenchman defending the fact that he speaks French.

SYLVIA. If he were speaking French, I'd like him much better.

PHILLIP. Well, I think that Sylvia might have a point.

SYLVIA. Thank you.

PHILLIP. That's not to say that I object to abstract expressionism per se. But if the subject of American art is in fact "The New," as Hughes posits, then how do you justify it's return, a mere thirty years after its flowering?

LILLIAN. It's American Neoclassicism. The only significant movement that was absolutely defined by American artists is, after all, abstract expressionism—

PHILLIP. Oh Lillian. Andy Warhol is spinning—

LILLIAN. I don't care; Pop Art was a dead end. The whole scene just turned into one huge disgusting crowd of poseurs and hypocrites, and I ought to know. People are hungry for art again, real art, beauty, truth, and everything else holy and good that got tossed out in the eighties. That's what we're going to give them.

LUCAS. You are so good.

LILLIAN. Thank you, and I've barely even begun. Mac and I are planning on making a ton of money, aren't we Mac?

KIDMAN. A ton of money. That sounds about right.

LUCAS. Careful, Mr. Kidman. You're very close to admitting that you very much care if people like your paintings after all.

KIDMAN. I only care if they buy them. The only one who has to like them is me.

LUCAS. Ah. A romantic distinction.

PHILLIP. Really, well, forgive me, but I think you'll care if the critics like them.

KIDMAN. *(Starting to lose it)* Yeah, okay—

PHILLIP. Am I wrong? Because from what we heard you

stopped showing because of one or two bad reviews—

KIDMAN. You don't know dick about it, asshole.

PHILLIP. Have I touched a nerve?

KIDMAN. *(To LILLIAN)* Who are these people?

LILLIAN. Leave the critics to me.

SYLVIA. You see, I was right. You care if the critics like you.

KIDMAN. Hey, I didn't ask to come here. I mean, this is horseshit—

LILLIAN. All right, Mac, thank you—

KIDMAN. This fucking homo trying to tell me something about my work. I mean—

PHILLIP. *(Outraged)* Excuse me? What did you call me?

LILLIAN. All right, that's enough! No more talk about art, or artists or critics. Let's talk about something else. Eugene—

EUGENE. *(Awaking from an ironic stupor)* Yes—

LILLIAN. Another topic, any topic.

LUCAS. Except poverty.

LILLIAN. Yes, except that.

EUGENE. Oh, all right. I was reading the other day about serial killers— *(All react.)* —Yes, and how psychologists have observed that these killers have actually driven themselves mad with self-loathing, and so the only time they're not in pain is when they're inflicting pain on others. The pleasure of murdering another human being is the only thing that makes life livable to them. And when I read this, I thought, my god, serial killers are just—critics. It's exactly the same thing.

(There is a terrible silence at this. KIDMAN suddenly roars with laughter.)

LILLIAN. *(Dry)* Thank you, Eugene.
EUGENE. You're welcome.

(Blackout)

Scene 10

(Kidman's apartment. JENNY sits at the table, trying to do homework for her G.E.D. class. WILLIE, her brother, is there bothering her. He is an entertaining jerk.)

WILLIE. So he's gonna do it? He's really gonna show? And you're gonna let him?

JENNY. Oh, like he listens to me.

WILLIE. This is insane. It's suicide. Do you remember what happened the last time?

JENNY. Of course I remember—

WILLIE. Jesus, Mom ended up in jail.

JENNY. It wasn't her fault.

WILLIE. Of course it wasn't her fault. It was all his fault. I'm just saying, Jesus. It's going to be a bloodbath. He's gonna show? What moron decided to give him a show?

JENNY. Some woman.

WILLIE. Is he screwing her?

JENNY. No. I don't know.

WILLIE. Do women still like him even? He's always

seemed so repulsive to me. Like some big disgusting cowboy. Why you stay with him, I will never understand.

JENNY. Somebody has to. He'll starve.

WILLIE. Good riddance. What a jerk. Remember when he got drunk and locked us in for three days? Remember that? What an asshole. Why do you stay here?

JENNY. It wasn't three days, it was one day.

WILLIE. It was one and a half days, because Charlie came up and heard us yelling and picked the lock. As you'll recall, Mac didn't come back for three entire days. He didn't know Charlie had picked the lock. As far as he was concerned, which wasn't very far—

JENNY. Willie, could you—god. I mean, I'm glad to see you, I am, but do you have to—

WILLIE. I'm just saying, Jesus. Look at this, you're still studying for your G.E.D., that's pathetic.

JENNY. Oh well, thank you, I appreciate the support.

WILLIE. I mean that in a good way. I mean, it's pathetic, he's feeding off you like some sort of giant bug, why don't you leave him? Come live with me. You're my sister, I love you, come live with me.

JENNY. You just want me to live with you because you hate him and you want him to starve.

WILLIE. Hey, if he starved, I'm not saying I wouldn't enjoy that. He's an asshole. He murdered Mom.

JENNY. He didn't—

WILLIE. Why do you defend him?

JENNY. I'm not defending him. It's just, you know, I was there too. I was there more than you. And I know he made a lot of mistakes, but Mom died of cancer, and I just don't—why can't her death just be hers? Why does it have to be part of him?

WILLIE. You don't think he had anything to do with her getting sick, and when he was too drunk to take her in for chemo—

JENNY. Oh god, Willie. Let's just have a good time, huh? I hardly ever get to see you. It's so great, you came over, and I just—I just don't want everything to always be about him.

WILLIE. That's what I'm saying. You shouldn't let him do this show. He'll be insufferable. And drunk. And then he'll get so worked up, we'll have to listen to him go on about the critics ad infinitum, ai yi yi—

JENNY. He's already started.

WILLIE. See? See?

JENNY. Please, he never stopped. Drinking, sometimes I can get him to stop drinking. But obsessing about the critics, no way.

WILLIE. Why do you stay with him?

JENNY. He's a really good painter.

WILLIE. That's not a reason.

JENNY. Do you want a drink?

(He looks up at this, startled. She grins at him.)

WILLIE. A drink?

JENNY. A gin and tonic. Would you like a gin and tonic?

WILLIE. A gin and tonic?

JENNY. Have you ever had one?

WILLIE. Yes I've had a gin and tonic. You don't drink.

JENNY. I drink. I started drinking; I drink gin and tonics. Do you want one?

WILLIE. I'm stunned.

(She finds gin and tonic in the refrigerator and starts making a couple drinks.)

JENNY. Oh why? Everybody in the world drinks. I got tired of not drinking. Everybody else just does whatever they wants, I should be able to have a drink once in a while.

WILLIE. No, of course, you were just so against it. You're so good.

JENNY. I don't want to be good anymore.

WILLIE. I don't think it's optional with you.

JENNY. I'm not saying I'm going to go out and, and start being mean to people.

WILLIE. Heaven forbid.

JENNY. I just want to relax a little. What's wrong with that?

WILLIE. Nothing. Does this mean you're going to start dating?

JENNY. Maybe.

(She hands him a drink.)

WILLIE. The entire west side just heaved a huge sigh of relief.

JENNY. *(Laughing)* Yeah, here's to it. *(They toast. There is a knock on the door. JENNY goes to answer it.)* Who's that? Charlie?

(EUGENE enters, carrying MAC. Both are drunk.)

EUGENE. It's me.

KIDMAN. *(Drunk)* This is a great guy, Jenny. You need to

talk to this guy. He's fantastic.

JENNY. Dad, would you—aww Jesus.

(She helps him sit, annoyed.)

EUGENE. Who are you?

WILLIE. Who are you?

JENNY. His name's Eugene. He's, his girlfriend is the woman who's giving Mac his show.

KIDMAN. What's that, gin? You're drinking gin? *(To EUGENE)* Let's have a drink.

WILLIE. Yes, have a drink. That's what you need. Because as usual you are nowhere near drunk enough.

KIDMAN. Shut up. You're never here, I don't have to listen to you.

JENNY. I'm here all the time. Will you listen to me?

KIDMAN. No. We saw the gallery, Jenny. It's amazing. It's amazing.

WILLIE. Yeah, I heard you were showing. What a great idea, Walter, that was so much fun for everyone, when you were doing that.

KIDMAN. Fuck you.

WILLIE. Fuck you too.

EUGENE. Who are you? *(To JENNY)* Who is this?

JENNY. This is my brother, Willie.

EUGENE. You have a brother?

JENNY. Of course I have a brother.

EUGENE. You never talk about him. *(To WILLIE)* They never talk about you.

WILLIE. They both wish I was dead.

JENNY. That is so not true!

KIDMAN. I wish he was dead.

WILLIE. Yeah, see, Mac wishes I was dead, and Jenny wishes I didn't wish Mac was dead. It evens out.

KIDMAN. *(Again on his own track, making drinks)* We went to the gallery. It's nice, it's not great—

EUGENE. But it's big. Bigger than it—

KIDMAN. *(Overlap, agreeing)* Bigger than it looks.

EUGENE. *(Overlap)* And we hung like six of them. It's—man, you should—

KIDMAN. *(Overlap)* Drinking and hanging paintings, you should see it, Jenny.

EUGENE. They look amazing.

KIDMAN. Amazing, right?

EUGENE. They look amazing.

JENNY. Dad, don't drink anymore.

(She tries to take the drink from him.)

KIDMAN. This was here! I didn't buy it!

JENNY. I bought it, I bought it for me, and—

KIDMAN. *(Amazed)* You're drinking? You shouldn't drink.

JENNY. You shouldn't drink.

KIDMAN. No no, I drink all the time.

JENNY. Dad, give me the drink.

KIDMAN. You're so good.

JENNY. I am not good.

EUGENE. Yes you are.

JENNY. I am not good!

KIDMAN. *(To WILLIE)* He thinks she's interesting.

WILLIE. I just bet he does.

EUGENE. *(Off JENNY, drunk)* She's interesting. What's so wrong, all I said was she's interesting.

JENNY. *(To EUGENE)* Could you leave, please? I have to get him to bed.

KIDMAN. No, no! He came to see you.

EUGENE. *(To KIDMAN)* I came to bring you home.

KIDMAN. Oh please. I been wandering this city drunk for more years than you were born. You shoulda seen it, Jenny. The gallery. They look great on those walls. You're gonna love it. I know you don't want me to do this, but they look great, the paintings look like, you know, fuck you! All of you, they look fucking amazing, and we are gonna make a ton of money, I'm gonna take you to Italy, Jenny— *(To WILLIE)* —Not you because she's the one who stuck it out, and I'm gonna take you to Italy and I'm gonna feed you pear number three, you think you know food, but you don't know food because you've never been to Italy, and we're gonna—you—we— *(His mood suddenly drops.)* I'm a piece of shit.

WILLIE. Oh, there's a newsflash.

JENNY. Willie.

KIDMAN. *(Brightening suddenly)* No, he's right. So what, I'm a piece of shit. Those are great fucking paintings, and they look great and you can quit your fucking day job, because I am going to make a ton of money. Do they look great or what?

(He laughs, delighted. He throws his arm around EUGENE, who laughs too at his sudden good humor. MAC takes Eugene's drink.)

EUGENE. They look fucking amazing.

JENNY. Don't give him that.

KIDMAN. You don't believe us? Believe me, darling, 'cause this time the truth will set you free. Those paintings are damn fucking good.

(He hugs her. She starts to laugh, finally infected by his mood.)

JENNY. I know, Dad, I've been telling you that for years—

KIDMAN. They're fucking great.

EUGENE. It's true. I've seen a ton of these shows, and this is a great show. It doesn't matter what the critics say.

KIDMAN. No, 'cause they're idiots. *(Laughing)* They're serial killers, that's what we figured out.

(EUGENE and KIDMAN are laughing.)

WILLIE. Well then you should all get along fine. Killing Mom, killing me, killing Jenny, you have much more in common than anyone thought.

JENNY. Willie—

WILLIE. I'm kidding! You have no sense of humor. You're too good.

JENNY. I'm not good!

KIDMAN. You are good, my sweetie pie. You're my good girl.

(He kisses her on the forehead, and then slumps on her. She helps him in a chair, and takes the bottle of gin from him.)

JENNY. Oh, Daddy.

EUGENE. He's all right.

JENNY. He's not all right. I mean, why do you think he's drinking like this? He's scared to death.

(She takes the glasses to the sink, annoyed now.)

EUGENE. No, you should have faith. It really is a great show. If he keeps his mouth shut and doesn't insult the wrong people, he'll be the next big thing.

WILLIE. So how much did he drink?

EUGENE. Not that much. Some, you know, wine with dinner, and some scotch, this gin here, then at the gallery people had, tequila, I think.

JENNY. Oh that's really great.

EUGENE. He's the one who brought it.

JENNY. And you just let him drink as much as he wanted.

EUGENE. Oh, you try telling him what to do.

JENNY. I do.

EUGENE. Yes, and I see how successful it is.

JENNY. You should go. Could you just go? Willie, give me a hand. *(She goes to MAC and tries to help him stand.)* Come on, Daddy.

(He slumps over.)

EUGENE. I'll help.

JENNY. It's fine.

EUGENE. Come on, let me help.

WILLIE. It's not fine, Jenny. *(He has picked up a cellophane*

*packet which fell out of Mac's pocket. JENNY looks over, star-
tled, as WILLIE looks in MAC's face.)* Come on, Dad, what is
this stuff?

JENNY. What is it?

WILLIE. I don't know. Come on, Mac, talk to me.

*(But MAC is completely out. He slumps to the floor. WILLIE tries
to hold him up. JENNY looks at the pills, horrified.)*

JENNY. What is this? What is this?

EUGENE. *(Startled)* I don't know. I didn't—I don't know
where he got that.

JENNY. Call nine one one.

EUGENE. I didn't know.

JENNY. Call, would you call? *(Desperate, WILLIE looks for
the phone. Continuing; to MAC)* Dad? Come on, Dad. Talk to
me, Dad. Daddy?

WILLIE. Where's the damn phone?

JENNY. Come on, Dad. Oh no. Daddy, come on. Please.

*(She holds him.
Blackout)*

End of Act I

ACT II

Scene 11

(Charlie's apartment. One of Ray's friends is there, completely comatose from the crack they are both smoking. The microwave is gone. Ray takes a hit off the crack pipe.)

RAY. If Negroes were actually citizens, we wouldn't have a racial problem. There is going to be a racial explosion. The only solution now is complete separation between the black race and the white race. Just as the white man has the right to defend himself, we have the right to defend ourselves. We don't hate him. We love ourselves. For the white man to ask the black man why do you hate us, is like the wolf asking his victim, do you like me? The white man is in no moral position to ask us anything.

JORDY. *(Mumbling)* Yeah, okay.

RAY. Look at you. Your sorry white ass wasted on crack, nobody in their right mind be smoking this shit no more, but here's you and me suckin' it down, what you think's gonna happen if we get busted on this? You get sent to rehab and I'm back on Rikers for selling it to you.

JORDY. *(Correcting him)* I sold it to you.

RAY. I'm talking white man's logic, fool. White man goes down on an OD, everybody talks what a tragedy, big fucking articles in the newspapers. This happened right here, I'm talking right in this building, piece of shit white man gets himself fucked up on pills and booze and everyone's all upset. Black man OD's, you think it's gonna show up in the papers? More like they try to arrest his dead ass. Dead white man, he's in the newspaper, meanwhile I'm still on parole for a job I didn't even do.

JORDY. You did that job.

RAY. That's not the point. I'm trying to tell you something.

JORDY. And I'm trying to tell you, you're full of shit, and you know why? Because O.J. walked.

RAY. You want to talk to me about O.J.?

JORDY. I don't want to talk about O.J.

RAY. You want to talk about O.J.?

JORDY. I don't want to talk about O.J.

RAY. 'Cause in case you failed to notice, O.J. was found innocent in a court of law. That man is a hero and I'm not saying he didn't do it, what I am sayin', he got himself a fair trial, which is something that has hitherto been denied to the black man. The only way the black man can earn respect in a white man's world is by having money, and that is what O.J. knew, and he stood up before this entire nation and said, I'm not your nigger, I am a rich man and I am going to buy me some justice, just like you white men been doing for hundreds of years. That is what O.J. did. And don't get me started on Nicole, 'cause that's not to say she wasn't asking for that shit—

JORDY. Aw come on, I don't want to talk about O.J!

RAY. Yeah, white people don't want to talk about O.J. 'cause they don't like to hear the truth.

JORDY. Fuck the truth, Ray. Come on.

(JORDY offers him the pipe.)

RAY. There's gonna be a race war. Count on it. Now, gim-mee that. *(RAY takes it and takes a hit.)* This is good shit.

JORDY. It is indeed.

(They laugh.
Blackout)

Scene 12

(Jenny's apartment. EUGENE is there, talking to CHARLIE.)

EUGENE. How is she?

CHARLIE. Not so good. Well, you know. It's a shock for everybody. I don't know what I'm thinking half the day.

EUGENE. Yes.

CHARLIE. All those years he was just a wild man, this never happened. Don't seem right, things finally looking up. You were here, they said.

EUGENE. Yes.

CHARLIE. They said he went real fast.

EUGENE. Yes.

CHARLIE. Yeah, that's what they said.

EUGENE. I'm here... I have something for Jenny.

CHARLIE. *(Awkward)* She said nobody but me and Willie. Plus she's sleeping, I don't...

EUGENE. Of course. *(Explaining, awkward)* It's just, she's

going to need money. Funerals, and the hospital, emergency rooms are expensive. Death is expensive.

(He holds out a check.)

> CHARLIE. I don't think she's gonna take that.
> EUGENE. It's hers.
> JENNY. Hey, Charlie, it's okay, I'll talk to him. *(She stands in the doorway, sleepy, looking at the men. She clutches a sweater, which she wears over a nightgown.)* What is that?
> EUGENE. It's from the show. The paintings, some of them were pre-sold. This is your money. I just thought, you'll probably need it.

(She steps forward and looks at the check, confused.)

> JENNY. The show isn't until next week.
> EUGENE. Tonight, actually, it's tonight. *(A beat, explaining again)* But some of the paintings are sold already. It's something the galleries do sometimes; they let important collectors come before the opening when there's a sense that it's potentially a big show.

(He is increasingly embarrassed. JENNY is confused.)

> JENNY. What do you mean, a big show? How would they know? No one knew who he was.
> EUGENE. *(Apologetic)* They know these things. There's a machinery. Publicists, you know.
> JENNY. *(Ignoring him)* Yeah, but this can't be right. Look at

this, Charlie, this is a lot of money.

(She shows the check to CHARLIE.)

CHARLIE. They paid that for Mac's paintings?

EUGENE. Actually, that's only fifty percent. That's Mac's cut. It's your money.

JENNY. Well, I don't need that. I'd rather have the paintings back.

(She puts it on the table.)

EUGENE. The paintings are sold.

JENNY. So, give them their money back.

CHARLIE. Can I get my picture back?

EUGENE. I don't think you understand. This is an important event. What's happened? The show is an important show.

JENNY. Oh yeah, now he's important, now that he's dead.

(She sits, miserable.)

CHARLIE. You want anything, honey? How 'bout I fix you a sandwich?

JENNY. Maybe some water would be good. I don't know. *(She looks around, honestly perplexed.)* Doesn't it seem weird, he's not here? It's like, I can't believe how much it looks like the same place. Look, the walls, they're the same walls, and the door is the same door. That night, when we came back from the hospital, I found a tube of paint behind the coffee machine. Burnt Umber. He dropped it there, sometimes, he would get in the middle of something and then go for something else and lose his paint. You know, he did that. So his paint's still here. I can't quite figure it out.

EUGENE. Jenny. You're going to need somebody to help you.

JENNY. Help me what?

EUGENE. Things are going to start to happen.

JENNY. *(On a different track again.)* I don't understand why I can't get those paintings back. I mean, what's the point, he's not here, what's the point of having the show?

EUGENE. The paintings have been sold. People think he's important.

JENNY. Stop saying that. He wasn't important when he was alive. He's not allowed to be important now.

CHARLIE. Don't talk about it sweetie.

JENNY. *(Starting to cry)* Charlie.

CHARLIE. It's okay, sweetie. *(He goes to her. To EUGENE)* You want to help, go see if you can get those paintings back.

EUGENE. I don't think I can.

CHARLIE. Mine looks like a duck.

(They both look at him, miserable.)

EUGENE. *(Beat; defeated)* I'll see what I can do.

(Blackout)

Scene 13

(Lillian's office. She is on the phone. EUGENE sits before her.)

LILLIAN. *(To EUGENE)* Is she insane? *(On the phone)* No, not you, Ivan. I know, that's—yes, I'll be there, I'LL BE THERE I just have to take care of this. Do not let *The Times* go, I need to talk to that guy. *(Another line rings)* Just a minute. *(She beeps it.)* Hello. Hi, Sy. Yes, it's stunning, it's really an astonishing show and it's such a tragedy what happened, the timing was just hideous, not that there's ever a good time to die, God, I sound so, but how can you ever talk about death without sounding like an idiot? I just, he was a personal friend and I really feel wretched. Yes, I know, Fred came by last week, and—I wish I could—yes, of course there are, he's been painting for years in obscurity, his loft is—I don't know, the daughter is desolate and it's just not clear what her plans are, much too soon, but as soon as I know I'll call you. Yes. This week. I'll—*(Three lines beep at once.)* Sy, I've got to go, the place is a zoo. Yes, this week. *(She hangs up, interjects to EUGENE)* Fuck him. I told him two weeks ago this was going to happen, it's not my fault he didn't—hello. *(She picks up another line.)* Ivan, I'll be there. Just give me three minutes. Look, we know it's a rave; that's not going to change if I make him wait for three minutes. *(She hangs up, grabs the other line.)* Ivan, I'll be there! *(She hangs up, continuing her rant to EUGENE) Vanity Fair* wants to do a major profile, they're talking to Dominick Dunne. Every major art critic is raving, the value of those fucking paintings tripled overnight, and she wants them BACK? That is not a realistic position, and I know she's in pain, god knows we're all devastated, but this is no time for sentimentality! Neal Costello is on the verge of offering him a retrospective at MOMA, which is astonishing given that the damn show hasn't even been reviewed yet, and in case you didn't notice, the fucking *New York Times* gave him a picture with an obit written by Robert Hughes himself, hasn't it even occurred to anybody that that didn't just happen? Mac isn't here to see this, well, he's going to get his moment in the sun just the same and it's not like I'm just doing this for myself by the way, so you just stop glowering at me like—

EUGENE. *(Overlap)* If I'm glowering, it's because you haven't given me a moment to get a word in edgewise! *(The phone suddenly rings again. Angry)* Do you think you could put that thing on hold and talk to me for just one minute?

(She does. She looks at him.)

LILLIAN. I'm sorry. But as you can see, a lot is happening, very quickly, and if I don't take care of this, now, someone truly hideous is going to step in and exploit the whole thing.

EUGENE. That's hardly a reason for you to exploit it.

(Beat)

LILLIAN. You find this grotesque.

EUGENE. Yes, I find it grotesque! You need to slow down. That poor girl is devastated—

LILLIAN. Well, that "poor girl" might try thinking about her father for once—

EUGENE. Don't start on her.

LILLIAN. Don't you start. I've been very patient about her, Eugene. After all. She's a cater-waiter who didn't even finish high school, and you tried to pick her up at our engagement party. And it's ridiculous, you thinking I didn't know.

(Beat)

EUGENE. Nothing happened.

LILLIAN. I know nothing happened. I know. *(Upset, she reaches into her purse, searching for something, drops a prescription bottle.)* I have such a migraine. I'm only saying, this is exactly what he was eating himself up about all those years; this is it. This is what he wanted, and I'm the one who got it for him. And she is not going to fuck it up!

EUGENE. She just doesn't understand—

LILLIAN. Don't explain her to me. Please. I will take it from here. I will let her know that she's not getting her paintings back; the paintings that are here in the gallery are off the table. What is now in negotiation is the rest of the collection. She's sitting on millions, for God's sake, and I'm not talking a few millions. I'm talking many, many millions.

(EUGENE starts to hand the bottle to her, then stops and looks at it.)

EUGENE. You just had this filled last week.

LILLIAN. And things have been a little tense since then, and now I have to have it filled again. *(She takes it back from him and shoves it into her purse. She kisses him.)* Now please, can you please go out and keep Ivan calm for just a few more minutes?

That call is still holding. *(EUGENE nods, considers her for a beat, and goes. She picks up the phone.)* Hello? Yes, hi, hi, I meant to call you back, but things are just crazy. I know. It's not clear what's going to happen, the daughter is very confused right now. No, I know, but I truly don't think it's going to be a problem. There's also a son.

(Blackout)

Scene 14

(Jenny's apartment. The light is on. KIDMAN sits at the table, reading the newspaper and eating a donut. JENNY enters the room and sees him. He looks up.)

KIDMAN. Did you see this? This guy compares me to Van Gogh. I'm an abstract expressionist, you fucking moron! Van Gogh painted flowers!

JENNY. Daddy.

KIDMAN. *(Reading)* Christ, this stuff is unbelievable. I mean, it's like all of a sudden I invented painting. Schnabel's just shitting, you know he is. Trust me, he's eating his own liver out. Oh yeah here we go, Basquiat. Yeah, our work is so similar.

JENNY. Daddy!

KIDMAN. What?

JENNY. I can't believe you came back from the dead to read

your reviews.

KIDMAN. *(Of course)* Good reviews?

JENNY. Am I the only person in this whole city who doesn't care about those things?

KIDMAN. I think you are, babe.

JENNY. Great.

KIDMAN. Hey, come on. Somebody writes about you in the newspaper—for instance let's say maybe The Biggest Newspaper In The World—it's a temptation to at least check it out. Christ, this stuff is tedious as shit. How come the most boring people on the planet get to write for the newspapers? I mean, I sat in this apartment for years making one pithy fucking brilliant observation after another, no one put that in the newspaper. Listen to this—

JENNY. *(Cutting him off)* Do you mind? I'm really not interested.

(KIDMAN sets the newspapers down, considers her.)

KIDMAN. So how's your lovely brother?

JENNY. Willie? He's fine. Busy. I haven't seen much of him since the funeral.

KIDMAN. Want to know why? He's out there, selling my paintings.

JENNY. *(Confused and surprised by this)* He can't—he can't sell them without me.

KIDMAN. Hey, he's out there doing it! It's done. And I don't want him to get the money. I want you to get the money. You're the one who stuck it out. He doesn't get shit out of this. I don't care if he is your brother.

JENNY. Would you stop calling him "your brother" like I created him? He's your son.

KIDMAN. Don't remind me, he's a total piece of shit.

JENNY. He is not! He's, what do you expect, anyway, you were such a lousy father, what do you expect?

KIDMAN. *(A gentle rebuke)* Jenny. Sell the paintings.

JENNY. No.

KIDMAN. I want you too.

JENNY. Well, I don't want to.

KIDMAN. Goddammit! That's my life in there—

JENNY. It's my life too, dad. I am the only person, I kept you going, all those years everyone told you it was shit, and now it's like oh big deal, that's your problem Jenny, none of it was true, that it didn't matter what they all said, it mattered, it's the only thing that did. And now everyone just wants, but that's what I did, with my life, and I know it was stupid, everyone keeps telling me how stupid I've been, but what was I SUPPOSED TO DO, let you die? I told you not to drink, I told you so many times and I know, I'm too good, well, I'm the one who bought the damn—it's my fau—I bought that, you were drinking, that night, if I didn't have that here.

(Beat)

KIDMAN. Oh, Jenny.

JENNY. *(Immediately defensive)* No. It's not my fault. You killed yourself, you son of a bitch. You couldn't be bothered to try and live, for me, because I needed you, that didn't even occur to you. You just went right ahead and killed yourself. Well, you're dead now so you don't get everything you want anymore!

I'm not selling those paintings.

KIDMAN. Whoa, wait a minute. You're trying to punish me?

JENNY. Why not? It's a good a reason. Maybe it's the best. You want to be famous after you're dead? Well, guess what, that's not gonna happen unless I feel like it, and I'm in a bad mood these days.

KIDMAN. You sell those paintings.

JENNY. No.

KIDMAN. You little bitch.

JENNY. Yeah, and you're an asshole.

KIDMAN. It won't make you happy.

JENNY. You don't care if I'm happy! You never cared. You just did what you wanted. You didn't give a shit about me.

KIDMAN. *(Simple)* That is not true.

JENNY. Why don't you go away? Just go away. You're not here anyway. Are you?

(Beat)

KIDMAN. No.

JENNY. Then go away.

(She starts to sob. He leaves. As he goes, he picks up the newspapers. She sits alone at the table sobbing. She falls asleep. The lights change; it is morning. CHARLIE enters. He brings the bird, and a coffee pot.)

CHARLIE. Rise and shine, sweet pea. Jenny, sweetie. Brung you breakfast.

*(He touches her on the shoulder. She sits up and looks around.
After a moment, she looks at CHARLIE.)*

JENNY. Charlie.

CHARLIE. You sleep out here? You hurt your neck, doing that.

JENNY. *(Sleepy, curious)* You brought your bird.

CHARLIE. Thought you might like the company. Yeah, she's a real good bird.

JENNY. You can't give me your bird.

CHARLIE. Not to keep, just for a little while. I come up here, I can visit her, watch some TV with you, that's what I thought. Brought you some coffee, too.

(He turns on a light and bustles about. He offers her a bagel from a bag.)

JENNY. *(Taking it)* Did something happen to your new TV?

CHARLIE. Oh no, it's fine. Real nice. Here you go.

JENNY. Then why do you want to come up here, our TV is terrible.

CHARLIE. Just for the company, sweetheart, that's what I meant.

JENNY. Charlie.

(He hesitates. She waits for his answer.)

CHARLIE. Ray took it, I guess.

JENNY. *(Disappointed)* He sold your TV?

CHARLIE. Got the microwave, too. *(A joke)* Now's he

lookin' at Swee'pea funny, I didn't want to take any chances.

JENNY. Look, we have some money around here some-where, they gave me that big check. Let's go buy you a TV set.

CHARLIE. No no.

(She finds the check.)

JENNY. Yeah, why not. I don't have anything to do with this, now that Mac's not here. Let's buy you another TV set. It would make me feel better.

CHARLIE. We could buy you a TV set.

JENNY. I don't watch TV.

CHARLIE. Everybody watches TV.

JENNY. I don't want a TV. I want you to have a TV.

CHARLIE. Well, let's just wait, then. You buy me another TV, Ray's just gonna sell that one, too.

(She sighs, sets the check down and checks the bagel.)

JENNY. What is this, lox spread?

CHARLIE. Yeah, I know that's your favorite.

JENNY. *(Starting to eat)* This is excellent.

CHARLIE. Only the best for you, honey.

JENNY. You shouldn't be spending your money on me. And you should kick Ray out. Selling your TV. It's not right.

CHARLIE. He's my sister's boy, Charlotte. She's a nice person, worked hard her whole life trying to keep him out of trou-ble. I hate to give up on him on account she's his mama. When I come back from the war, she used to just sit with me for days. Everybody else acting like you gotta get over this now, and

here's this nine year old girl just willing to sit. It meant something, you know. I don't like to talk about the war now, but after-
wards, you feel so beat down, like every one of us, not even that
you don't have a soul, but if you do, it's a evil thing, and this
world needs to spit us out. All that killing teaches you what a
man's worth and that's the sad truth. Then there's this little girl,
just sitting there, waiting for me to say something, day after day.
Sometimes we'd take a walk. And I started thinking, there's another side to things. Can't put a price on a life. We're worth more
than killing alone. That's what she give me. And now, she got so
much hope sunk into that boy, I just hate to give up.

(He joins her, eating the bagel.)

  JENNY. Well maybe if he got a job. That would help.
  CHARLIE. It's hard, black man with a record. Least if he's
gonna steal, he's only stealing from me, that's the way I look at
it, 'cause honestly, he is not a very good thief. You know how
they caught him? He's breaking and entering this dry cleaning
operation after hours, climbs down a empty chimney they had
there. Then he breaks open the cash register, takes what's there,
which ain't much, looks around, can't find the safe, 'cause it's
not even on the property, realizes this is all he's gonna get, sev-
enty-two fifty, something like that, so he gets mad. Finds a crow-
bar and trashes the place for kicks, just 'cause he's in a bad mood
now, right? So then he goes to the back door, looking to take off?
It's locked. Front door's locked too! He can't get out! Tries to
climb back out the chimney, gets stuck. All night! He's in there
so long he pees his pants! They find him in there, the next day,
yelling help me, help me! Four years, breaking and entering. That

boy is not bright. *(JENNY laughs. CHARLIE smiles at her.)* Four years. For a robbery he didn't even finish? I don't mind he took my television. I'm just back where I started, that's the way I figure it. Serves me right, selling Mac's painting like that. Sure wish I still had that.

(JENNY reaches over and takes his hand, grateful.)

JENNY. You want one? I'll give you one.

CHARLIE. Oh no, sweetie.

JENNY. He would want you to have one.

CHARLIE. He already give me one, and I sold it to that woman, and if I didn't, he maybe would still be here. I know it's stupid to think things like that, but sometimes you can't help it.

(He smiles at her, a sad acknowledgement.)

JENNY. Take a painting. Please.

CHARLIE. Those things are worth something. You can't just be giving 'em away.

JENNY. Why not?

CHARLIE. Well, because it'd be nice to have a little money for once! All those years, you working so hard, keeping things together for Mac. Wouldn't you like a little rest?

JENNY. You just told me your only regret was selling Mac's painting, and now you're telling me that's what I should do? Charlie.

CHARLIE. Yeah, that don't make much sense, do it?

(They smile at each other. The door opens; WILLIE enters.)

WILLIE. Hey.
JENNY. Willie!
CHARLIE. Hey Willie.

(She hugs him.)

JENNY. Where have you been?
WILLIE. So, come live with me, you'll see me more. You're never here. He's dead now. Come live with me.
JENNY. Do you want some coffee?
WILLIE. Yeah, okay. How have you been? Are you all right?
JENNY. I don't know, Willie, it's all been so—I think I'm making myself a little nuts, stuck in here. I'm so glad you came by. Can you stay? There's bagels, too. Here, you can have some of mine. Lox spread.
WILLIE. Jenny, we have to talk about the paintings.

(She stops at this, looks at him.)

JENNY. What about them?
WILLIE. We have to talk about who is the best person to handle them.
JENNY. What do you mean, "handle?"
WILLIE. Sell. Who we want to sell them for us. *(She looks away.)* I've been down to the gallery, several times, and I've talked to a lot of different people, and I really think we should let Lillian continue to take care of this. She's clearly, she's absolutely as professional as anyone out there; she knew Mac, she loves the paintings—

JENNY. *(Bitter)* None of this would have happened if she hadn't come along in the first place.

WILLIE. Look, Mac did what he wanted to do. This was what he wanted.

JENNY. *(Angry now)* Yeah, I know. I know, okay? But I don't care. Nobody's gonna "handle" anything, because I'm not selling anything.

(Beat)

WILLIE. Do you know how much they're worth now? Millions. Many millions.

CHARLIE. How much?

WILLIE. That's right. This is a good thing, and I'm not going to let you pretend that it's not. Our whole lives have changed. You can move out of this shithole, finish your G.E.D. and go to college. You can take a trip if you want. Mac wanted to take you to Italy? Go to Italy. He would want you to go to Italy!

JENNY. He doesn't get what he wants anymore. He's dead.

WILLIE. But you're not. And neither am I. I'm telling you, honestly, when all this started to happen, I admit I was not immediately thrilled. I mean, there's no point in my lying about it; I wasn't Mac's biggest fan. But you know what? All this hooha, Mac's suddenly a genius, you know what I decided? I can live with it. You always wanted me to forgive him, I can do that. You want me to be his son? I'll be his son. I'll tell everybody whacky stories about what a crazy nut he was. What a whacky genius. And you know what? They'll pay me for the stories. They'll pay you for the stories. And they'll pay us both for those goddamn paintings.

JENNY. I'm not selling the paintings, Willie! Are you listening to me? I'm not selling them! We are not selling them!

(They stare at each other.)

CHARLIE. Well, I guess I better...

JENNY. Charlie, no, stay here, this isn't anything. This discussion is over. Please. Go, take a painting. I want you to have one.

WILLIE. What?

JENNY. I told Charlie he could have a painting! Is that all right with you?

WILLIE. I'm standing here begging you to let go of the damn things and he gets to just walk off with one?

JENNY. You want to sell them!

WILLIE. Yes, I do! They're mine now, I—

JENNY. They're not yours!

WILLIE. They're half mine. I'll take half.

JENNY. You're not taking any.

WILLIE. So he gets one and I don't get any.

CHARLIE. I don't—

JENNY. Yes. Yes! He loved Mac. He loves those paintings. You don't.

WILLIE. I love you! Doesn't that count?

(There is a terrible pause at this. JENNY cannot answer for a moment. WILLIE turns away, shaking his head.)

JENNY. Of course it does. Of course. I'm sorry, I'm so confused. I don't mean to be like this. I'm sorry. *(He goes to her.*

JENNY embraces him.) I'm sorry. It's so hard. It's so hard, to know how to be, and you haven't been here—

WILLIE. I'm sorry. I thought I was doing the right thing; I knew you wouldn't want to deal with all this—it's chaos; it is chaos, and I was trying to take care of it so you didn't—

JENNY. *(Overlap)* I know. I know, you're right, it's just— maybe if you took one, Willie, just for now, just one.

WILLIE. *(Gentle)* Jenny, one is not going to be enough. They want all of them—

JENNY. Well, they can't have all of them, they—Okay, look. I'll give you one, and you can sell it, and it'll be worth a lot, Willie, they'll give you a lot for that, and, and—

WILLIE. You have to give me more than one, Jenny.

JENNY. *(Suddenly losing it)* I don't have to give you any! You're just gonna sell it, it's just money to you, it's just MONEY.

(She turns away from him, at a loss. Both CHARLIE and WILLIE are stunned into silence at her outburst.)

CHARLIE. Willie, maybe now is not the best time.

WILLIE. Don't you tell me what to do here. This is not your business.

JENNY. It is his business. He is as much a part of this—

WILLIE. No, he's not! You and I were the ones who lived through it, every sorry, miserable sordid fucking moment of that man's misery, Mom's death, you and I were the end result—

JENNY. And the paintings.

WILLIE. They're not a person! They're nothing! He sat in that room and scribbled self-indulgent bullshit for thirty years, while he was also, by the way, ruining our lives, and now all of a sudden, people are saying that scribble is worth a zillion dollars, well, I want the money! Now, I'm sorry Mac's dead, not because I'm really sorry, but I'm sorry for you. Okay? I'm sorry because I know you loved him, and I know you're in pain, but I didn't get what you got from him. We all know that. He loved you, and he didn't love me, and he owes me now. And I'm taking those paintings.

(She doesn't answer. They stare at each other, immovable.)

CHARLIE. *(Trying to mediate)* It's too soon, maybe. Hey, Willie? Maybe it's just too soon.

WILLIE. *(Near tears)* Jenny. Let me have the paintings.

(She shakes her head. CHARLIE stands there, awkward.)

CHARLIE. Maybe in a little while. Hey Willie. It's just too soon.

*(After a moment, WILLIE turns and goes.
Blackout)*

Scene 15

*(Sylvia's apartment. Another dinner party. EUGENE, LILLIAN,
LUCAS and PHILIP are there. LILLIAN and EUGENE are
arguing.)*

LILLIAN. *(Heated)* It's just that this situation with MOMA
could not be more out of hand, and if you honestly think—
EUGENE. *(Overlap)* I realize that, Lillian, but I have been as
clear as I know how to be about this—
LILLIAN. *(Overlap)* That I would be asking, although why
I am not, in this situation, permitted to ask for a little bit of
help.
EUGENE. *(Overlap)* That I do not want to be involved. I
simply do not want any part of this!
LILLIAN. *(Overlap)* If not for me, then for Mac. You were
fond of him. I just don't understand why you can't do this for
Mac.

*(This finally silences him. The others look back and forth, a little
alarmed.)*

SYLVIA. My goodness, a battle royale!
LILLIAN. I'm sorry. I'm sorry, Sylvia.

*(She leaves the table momentarily, to collect herself. PHILIP and
LUCAS take this in.)*

SYLVIA. Oh don't apologize, that was very exciting. And I

have to say, I'm on your side. I think Eugene is being a cad about this.

EUGENE. A cad?

SYLVIA. Well, not very nice then. Why shouldn't you pitch in a little. She's working so hard, and all she's asking is that you make a few phone calls. Isn't that it?

LILLIAN. It's all right, Sylvia.

SYLVIA. It's not, oh. Look how unhappy she is. Your bride-to-be. Why won't you help her?

PHILLIP. It's money again.

EUGENE. It's not money.

SYLVIA. Well, what is it?

EUGENE. I don't know, Mother, I don't—

SYLVIA. Well, she doesn't have time for you to be confused. She needs your help now.

LILLIAN. Eugene. Just because—

EUGENE. Could we not discuss this here?

LILLIAN. Just because people are now willing to pay for those paintings doesn't mean they've been corrupted. All it means is that people with money have come to recognize what I recognized months ago: The paintings are good. And I just don't think it's wise to get sucked into some impossibly romantic position, that they were somehow "better" when no one was willing to buy them. It's a ridiculous idea, Eugene. It just is. Mac would have tossed it back in your face.

EUGENE. I know he would have.

SYLVIA. Now wait a minute. Is he arguing that those paintings are worth more if no one will pay for them?

EUGENE. I'm not arguing anything.

LUCAS. Sooo ... you're helping?

(They all stare at him.)

EUGENE. I will talk to her.

LILLIAN. That's all I ask.

SYLVIA. Oh good, we're all friends again. Although I have a confession to make about those paintings. I still don't like them! Well, I'm not saying I don't like them. I don't like them, but it's not that I don't like them a lot. It's just that I don't love them. I like them a little. I just don't know what to think now. All right, I'm just going to say it. I don't care that everyone likes them so much. I still don't like them.

LUCAS. You just don't understand them, Sylvia. That's different.

SYLVIA. Are you sure? Because I think I don't like them.

PHILLIP. Abstract expressionism is a very intellectual taste. It's not for everybody.

SYLVIA. I'm intellectual. I hope you're not saying I'm not intellectual.

PHILLIP. No no, of course—

LUCAS. *(Overlap)* No, that's not at all—I think you actually like them, you just don't know it.

EUGENE. Oh, for god's sake—

SYLVIA. Stay out of this, Eugene, please! I'm trying to understand, I want to share in everyone's—everyone's so excited, and I just, I'm sorry but he was so—you didn't really like him, did you?

LUCAS. Who, Kidman? Well, he was difficult—

PHILLIP. He was a homophobe. There, I said it.

SYLVIA. Precisely. He insulted people.

LILLIAN. He had his demons, no one is denying that.

PHILLIP. Oh please, demons. If anyone else had acted like that you would just come out and call him a bigot.

LILLIAN. Yes, and Picasso was a misogynist, and Eliot was an anti-Semite and D.W. Griffiths was a racist. But they were also gifted, and so we look the other way. *(Lillian's cell phone rings. She answers it.)* Ivan—*(To the others)* Sorry, I'm so sorry, really, I'll be right—

(She leaves the group as they continue their debate. EUGENE watches her, worried.)

LUCAS. Well, I suppose the only thing to conclude is, you can enjoy an artist and appreciate his work and still not want to have dinner with him.

SYLVIA. There. That's what I mean. I mean, I feel terrible even, the man is dead after all—

PHILLIP. Sylvia, he was rude to you; he was, and no one expects you to forget that. But the paintings are a different matter.

SYLVIA. *(To LUCAS)* So you actually like them?

LUCAS. They're magnificent.

PHILLIP. They are, Sylvia. We both need to put our feelings about the man aside and just appreciate them apart.

SYLVIA. Apart from the painter, as if someone else painted them.

PHILLIP. Yes. Someone you like. Lucas. What if Lucas painted them?

SYLVIA. Well, if Lucas painted them I would like them because he painted them and he's my friend and I would think oh how wonderful, that I have such talented friends, and I'd throw a big party to celebrate your grand success.

LUCAS. Thank you.

SYLVIA. I wish Lucas had painted them, it would be so much easier on me. Or Eugene, if Eugene had painted them, I'd be the mother of the artist, wouldn't that be fun.

EUGENE. Oh my god.

SYLVIA. Well, why shouldn't I think that would be fun? All you do is sit around and mope about having so much money. At least if you were an artist, I'd have something to be proud of.

(There is an uncomfortable beat while everyone tries not to notice what she just said.)

LILLIAN. *(Snapping)* Ivan, I cannot deal with this now! *(Beat; to the others)* I'm sorry, really. I'm so sorry. *(To phone)* Tell him he'll get it, and I'll call him in the morning. *(She hangs up.)* Sorry. Where were we?

EUGENE. We were talking about art.

LILLIAN. Of course we were. Sylvia, you do like those paintings. I won't let you not like them.

(She takes her hand, firm.
Blackout)

Scene 16

(Kidman's apartment, night. EUGENE is there with JENNY.)

EUGENE. Thanks for seeing me.

JENNY. No, I was glad to get your note.

EUGENE. I tried calling.

JENNY. I unplugged the phone. People keep calling, news-papers... I just unplugged it.

EUGENE. I don't blame you.

JENNY. *(A little awkward)* So, I was glad to get your note, and I'm glad you came. I've been meaning to thank you.

EUGENE. Thank me?

JENNY. For trying to get the paintings back. I mean, I know that was a crazy thing to ask for. And I never heard back from you. Well, of course, I did unplug the phone. But, thank you for trying.

EUGENE. I didn't—

JENNY. I know, but—

EUGENE. *(Abrupt, suddenly bitter)* Look, don't thank me, okay? I mean, we all know, I haven't been—look. It wasn't exactly your lucky day when you met me. I know that. I came onto you at my own—and I'm not apologizing for that, that was—and everything else, let's face it. I hunted you down. They probably would have found you anyway, but I was the one, I brought Lillian here, you knew that, I brought her here because I wanted to see you, and then that night, we were drinking, he was, and I knew it was too much and I knew it was a problem and I didn't stop it because I was thinking about you, and how I wanted to see you, and be his friend so I could come home with him, and see you. So don't thank me. Just don't thank me.

(Beat)

JENNY. It wasn't your fault.

EUGENE. *(Erupting)* I'm not asking for absolution! *(Beat)* I'm sorry, but this is--do you know what you're doing? Do you have any idea?

JENNY. *(Confused now)* No.

EUGENE. I told you, things were going to happen. I told you.

JENNY. What's happened?

EUGENE. They will not stop, do you understand that? You're being a fool! Just sitting here, like some sort of—if you rot in here with them, what will it prove? What will it prove? *(Beat. He looks at her.)* I'm sorry. I don't know what I'm...

JENNY. It's okay. It's not your fault.

(He shakes his head, at a loss, and prowls the apartment, looking about. She watches him, confused. He turns on her.)

EUGENE. *(Sudden)* Would you have dinner with me?

JENNY. Dinner?

EUGENE. Yes, I would like to do something for you. I haven't been able to do anything, and I keep thinking about that first night, when we met—you were so sad, and we were so hideous—and you were waiting on us. Like a servant.

JENNY. I was a servant.

EUGENE. Yes, you were, and you behaved better than anyone else in the room, and I would like to take you to dinner.

There are so many beautiful restaurants in this city, beautiful, where the food is like nothing you've ever tasted before, not even in your dreams—

JENNY. *(Smiling slightly)* Mac said the best food in the world is in Italy.

EUGENE. Oh, no no. I promise you, at this moment in history, food is taken very seriously in New York City, and Italy has been left in the dust. And I would like to take you to a restaurant, with chandeliers, flowers everywhere, staggeringly beautiful bouquets of—six people to wait on you alone. At your place setting, there will be twelve forks, and no one will know what any of them are good for—and there will be champagne, and sorbet, in between courses—to cleanse the palate, the flavors, one stranger than the next. Once, I had sorbet made out of parsley—

JENNY. *(Laughing)* That sounds terrible.

EUGENE. It was delicious. We will have it between the appetizer and the fish course.

JENNY. What will the appetizer be?

EUGENE. *(Thinking)* Oysters in a sauerkraut cream sauce topped with Beluga caviar.

(She laughs at this, delighted.)

JENNY. And dessert?

EUGENE. Chocolate crusted coconut sherbet, swimming in a lemongrass citrus soup. And that's just one of them. We'll order four. The other ones, I can't even begin to describe. If I tried, you would never believe another word out of my mouth.

(They smile at each other. He reaches out for her. They kiss. The

kiss becomes passionate. She pulls away.)

JENNY. This isn't right.
EUGENE. Jenny, maybe it's time you faced the fact that doing what's right hasn't gotten you anything that you wanted.

(He kisses her again. It starts to get quite heated. She pulls away.)

JENNY. We still have to make it through dinner.
EUGENE. Let's go.

(They do.
Blackout)

Scene 17

(Lillian's gallery. LILLIAN sits alone, by her desk, smoking a cigarette. She waits for a long moment. The phone rings. It rings again, and then again, and then again, as she considers it. Finally, she reaches forward and picks it up.)

LILLIAN. Hello?

(Blackout)

Scene 18

(Jenny's apartment. The lights are out. WILLIE sits there, alone, for a long moment. The door swings open. JENNY and EUGENE enter, kissing. They do not see him at first.)

WILLIE. Jenny.

(She turns, startled.)

JENNY. Willie—oh, man, what? You scared me.
WILLIE. We have to talk.
JENNY. What are you doing here?
WILLIE. We have to talk. He should go.

(He looks at EUGENE. There is a terrible pause.)

JENNY. What happened? Something happened.

(She looks around, uneasy. She looks at the door of the studio.)

WILLIE. Jenny—
JENNY. What did you do, Willie?
WILLIE. I took the paintings. Okay? I took the paintings.

(She looks at him in horror, then goes to the studio. WILLIE looks at EUGENE.)

EUGENE. You piece of shit.

WILLIE. Look, I'm not going to say anything about whatever it is you're doing here, but this is also none of your business, so—

JENNY. They're all gone. All of them, not one of them is— *(To Eugene)* Did you know he was doing this?

WILLIE. I did it, Jenny. I did it myself.

JENNY. You couldn't, there were too many of them, you had to—they're all gone, not one, you couldn't leave me one?

WILLIE. I did it for your own good—

JENNY. *(Losing it)* That is a FUCKING LIE, Willie, would you just—you took the paintings. *(A breath)* You took the paintings.

(She looks down, trying to stay somewhat on top of this.)

EUGENE. I'm calling the police.

WILLIE. That's not gonna do her any good, and you know it.

EUGENE. *(Pissed)* Yeah, I don't know anything of the kind, asshole, so—

WILLIE. *(Overlap)* I already talked to a lawyer, all right, and you know as well as I do, him dying in testate gives me a ton of rights in this situation. I mean, I didn't want to handle it like this. Jenny. You know I didn't. But you didn't leave me much choice.

JENNY. *(Trying to figure this out, upset)* How did you know? How did you know I was going out tonight, even I didn't—he just came over, and said dinner, I—you couldn't have known. And moving them all, they're all—where are they—he's gone. He's gone.

(She sobs for a moment, turns away. WILLIE goes to her, touches her shoulder.)

WILLIE. Jenny—

JENNY. Do not touch me! You are not allowed to touch me, Willie. No more. Don't ever try to touch me again.

(He looks at her, shattered.)

WILLIE. I did it for your own good.

JENNY. You did it because you're greedy.

WILLIE. Hanging onto those pictures is not going to bring him back.

JENNY. Don't talk to me about what I'm going through—

WILLIE. *(Overlap)* He died. He's gone. He maimed your life, he maimed mine, and he's dead now, and you need to try and figure out how to live.

JENNY. *(Overlap)* This isn't about me—you didn't do this for me!

WILLIE. Yeah, okay, fine, I did it for me. I admit it. I did it to get something back for me. I asked you, I begged you to come live with me. He got mom, and then he got you, and you have done nothing with your life. You're a cater waiter for god's sake! And you're sitting here like this is some fucking holy sepulcher, some tomb, some—you're my family too! I mean, what was it supposed to be, forever, I get nothing? He gets everything, and I— *(He stops himself. She shakes her head.)* I had every right to do what I did.

JENNY. I just needed more time. Why couldn't you—

WILLIE. We did not have time. It was happening now. Time

was the one thing I couldn't give you.

JENNY. You didn't even try. You took them all, all of them—that's not—that's mean, Willie. That's revenge.

WILLIE. That's not—I tried. God, I did nothing but—I begged you, and you wouldn't give me any, you wouldn't give me— why didn't I matter? Why—this is on you, Jenny. This is on you.

(He turns away, furious. She looks at his back, suddenly defeated.)

JENNY. I just couldn't do it. When it was just me and Mac, and the paintings, I just thought that was better. All those years, watching him paint, he was so—big. While he was painting? It was a sight to see. And they were so beautiful. I used to wonder where they came from; the color, and the light, it was such ... a gift. From, I didn't know where, but they were a gift. And I was a part of them. Then when he left, I just wanted to hang on to that sense that I did something, I—my life wasn't about money. It was a gift. That's all I was trying to do.

WILLIE. A gift to him, but not to me.

(A beat. She closes down.)

JENNY. You need to get out of here. You got what you wanted. Take the paintings, and take the money, and get out of here, and don't ever come back.

EUGENE. Jenny—

JENNY. Both of you. Leave me alone.

(She goes to her bedroom.
Blackout)

Scene 19

(Charlie's apartment. It is dark. RAY and JORDY are counting money.)

JORDY. No, come on, this ain't right.

RAY. That's right.

JORDY. You think I'm stupid?

RAY. I don't know you're some kind of genius, but that's not saying that ain't right.

JORDY. Hey Ray, you know what? You talk bullshit. And I'm six hundred short here.

RAY. Hey you want to count my split? 'Cause—

JORDY. Five thousand dollars, you said—

RAY. I said four—

JORDY. Fuck you, man. Don't you fuckin' talk to me like I'm a fuckin' moron!

RAY. It was my gig, I cut you in.

JORDY. I did all the fuckin' work.

RAY. Yeah, how you figure that? 'Cause my memory is I arranged the job, I got the truck—

JORDY. *(Overlap)* I figure that 'cause you and the skinny guy stood around chatting up old times while I was movin' that shit—

RAY. Bullshit, you a half-brain crackhead, your fuckin' problem—

JORDY. Fuck you—

(He pulls a knife. RAY looks at him, shocked. CHARLIE enters.)

CHARLIE. Hey, how's it goin'—hey. Whoa. Shit.

(The two younger men look over, startled.)

RAY. Hey, uncle Charlie.

CHARLIE. What's goin' on?

JORDY. I want my six hundred dollars. *(To CHARLIE)* He took six hundred dollars off me.

RAY. I never did.

CHARLIE. Put that thing away. I'm telling you, we are not having any sort of conversation here, till you put that thing away. *(JORDY pockets the knife. CHARLIE considers them both.)* Okay, Ray. Now why don't you tell me what you did.

RAY. I didn't do nothin'.

CHARLIE. *(To JORDY)* That right?

RAY. *(Reacting)* You gonna believe him, over me? Your own nephew, that's real nice. Mama gonna be real happy to hear about that—

CHARLIE. Don't you talk to me about your mama. *(Beat, to JORDY)* Now, you tell me what this is about.

JORDY. We did this job.

RAY. Whoa—that is not—

JORDY. Yeah, and you're a fuckin' liar, cause I heard you talking to that guy, agreement was five thousand dollars, and you stiffed me, man. I am six hundred short. Six hundred bucks. Short.

RAY. That is not—

JORDY. Yeah it is—

CHARLIE. Tell your friend to shut up because I'm talkin' to you now, you little piece of shit. *(CHARLIE suddenly grabs RAY, shoves him against the couch, reaches into Ray's pocket and takes out a wad of cash.)* Not enough you stealing from me, you doin' jobs now? You gonna break your mama's heart one more time, that what you're doing?

(He hurls him to the floor. RAY tries to crawl away.)

RAY. No way! It was a legit job! We moved those paintings! No stealing about it!

(CHARLIE stops, looks at him.)

CHARLIE. You stole Mac's paintings?

(They face off.)

RAY. I moved 'em. Willie told me about his sister goin' crazy, he needs to get them out of there. So that's what we did. I'm on the lookout, see when she takes off, give him a call, and we move 'em.

CHARLIE. *(Taking this in)* You stole Mac's paintings.

RAY. *(Protesting)* They ain't called the cops yet, and they ain't goin' to, Charlie. Them things half Willie's to begin with, and she ain't gonna want the trouble.

(RAY starts to pick up the money.)

CHARLIE. 'Cording to Willie.

RAY. That's right. Aside which, he gonna keep us out of it. Cops get involved, he did the whole thing himself. Better for him, better for us that way. I'm telling you, there is no downside here. Till this fool starts up with all his money negotiations.

CHARLIE. They catch you, how many years you back in for?

RAY. I told you, that ain't coming into it.

CHARLIE. Long as you can trust Willie. A white man. Any of it goes wrong, you really think he'll keep you out of it? 'Cause the way I see it, you put your freedom on the line for five thousand dollars.

RAY. Hey, don't you talk to me about money. A black man wants respect in this community, he got to have money, and I'm not talking minimum wage. You go get yourself shot up in Viet Nam, how much they give you for that, Charlie? Nine hundred dollars? Nine- thirty-two a month? You can't even buy yourself a TV set! Only way a black man earns respect, he got to have the cash. Then they listen. And now they gonna start listening to me.

CHARLIE. That's fine, Ray. That's a fine way to think about it. 'Cause way it looks to me? White man bought and sold you like a slave.

RAY. *(Stung by this)* Yeah, listen to you, tired old black man spends all his time running after some white girl. I mean, she's a nice piece of ass, but you honestly think she gonna be dishin' that honey your way? Then again, maybe you'll get lucky. 'Cording to Willie, she's a complete fuckin' nut job.

(Beat)

CHARLIE. You get out of my house. You get out of this neighborhood. I ever see you again, I'm sending you away.

RAY. You mean I don't get to sleep on your shitty little

couch no more? That really breaks my heart. *(Beat)* See ya
'round.

*(He goes.
Blackout)*

Scene 20

*(Sylvia's apartment. Another dinner party, with LUCAS, WILLIE,
LILLIAN, EUGENE and SYLVIA. Mac's painting is
there.)*

LUCAS. You just—took the paintings? You took them! Is
that legal?

SYLVIA. Oh, who cares if it was legal? It was bold, and
daring, and we applaud you!

WILLIE. *(Answering the question)* It was no more or less
legal than her refusal to give them up. I had to do something.

PHILLIP. Is she going to sue?

WILLIE. I don't know. It's unlikely.

SYLVIA. Well, that's too bad, because if you ask me, the
only thing further that we need, is a trial. Wouldn't that be fun?

WILLIE. Really, what I did, I did it for her own good. I
think, with time, she'll realize that. I think she may know it already.

(But he doesn't seem too sure. LILLIAN pats his hand.)

LILLIAN. You didn't just do it for her. You did it for Mac.
WILLIE. Oh—
LILLIAN. Don't be modest. We had many many talks about this, and Willie realized that time was of the essence and his father's legacy, to the world, was the most important consideration. It's true, Willie. What you did was very brave.
SYLVIA. Well, I'm happy things have finally settled down, because you seem like a very nice young man, but I feel that I must be forthright. I was not your father's biggest fan.
WILLIE. No?
SYLVIA. Oh, I love the paintings, of course I love the paintings, but frankly, I found him—difficult.
WILLIE. *(Confiding)* So did I.
SYLVIA. *(Relieved)* You didn't like him either. Thank god. But we mustn't judge an artist by the way he behaves. Phillip taught me that.
LUCAS. Well, when your sister feels better about the whole thing, I think we should invite her to dinner. To make the picture complete.
SYLVIA. What? Invite her? But she waited on us!
PHILLIP. Oh my god, I just put it together. That's the girl? The girl who was here, who went on and on about being poor?
SYLVIA. Yes and she's not poor anymore, and you'd think she'd be grateful, instead of just giving everyone so much trouble.
EUGENE. Maybe she just decided some things were worse than poverty.
LUCAS. *(Good natured)* Here we go again.

SYLVIA. Change the subject!

LILLIAN. Not at all. I'd like to hear what Eugene has to say.

EUGENE. Would you?

(There is a pause while they face each other from across the table. Their attitude toward each other is distinctly frosty.)

LILLIAN. Yes. Mac's retrospective opens in two weeks, advance word is stunning, his work will be seen alongside every major expressionist in every major museum in the world in the years to come, and if you think things could have worked out better, I think we'd all be interested in hearing how.

EUGENE. Do you really want me to answer that?

LILLIAN. Why don't you just tell us what's bothering you.

EUGENE. I just think there are loose ends.

LILLIAN. What kind of loose ends?

EUGENE. Questions. You know, after something terrible has happened, a death, everyone sits around and wonders, if I had only done something a little different, maybe this wouldn't have happened. We all blame ourselves.

SYLVIA. It's no one's fault.

EUGENE. I was drinking with him. Someone gave him those pills.

LILLIAN. It wasn't the pills that killed him. It was the pills and the alcohol and the years of sheer, pointless excess that killed him. *(To WILLIE)* Forgive me.

WILLIE. It's true. One way or another he was going to do himself in.

EUGENE. Other questions, then. You know, ever since that night, I've been wondering why, when you moved the paintings to the gallery, why'd you take all of them? I understand you were in a difficult situation, but it did seem pretty harsh. Why didn't you leave her just one?

WILLIE. *(Nervous now)* Well, actually I didn't—I wanted to. But Lillian—she said she needed to see them all.

EUGENE. Really? Why?

LILLIAN. They're important work. They had to be catalogued. She doesn't have proper security in that apartment, not to mention the dust, the heat, the humidity, it's a disastrous environment for fine art. There were many reasons.

EUGENE. Objective reasons.

LILLIAN. What other kind of reasons would there be?

EUGENE. I'm just asking questions, Lillian. It's my nature. Actually, both of us, that may be the reason we first fell in love. We're both the kind of people who look for answers. We sit, we watch, we think. Somehow, we always know what the other is doing.

SYLVIA. *(Joking)* Well, I don't know if that's such a good thing.

LILLIAN. It's neither bad nor good. It all depends on how one acts. Or doesn't.

EUGENE. On the basis of that knowledge.

LILLIAN. Yes.

SYLVIA. Well, now I don't understand what you two are talking about.

EUGENE. It's all right, mother, we understand each other. *(Standing)* I've got to go.

SYLVIA. Oh Eugene, you can't! We haven't had the savory yet.

EUGENE. I'm full, Mother. Lillian, you and I—this clearly

isn't working out.

LILLIAN. *(Cool as a cucumber)* No, clearly not.

EUGENE. So that's it then.

LILLIAN. Yes.

(The others look around, surprised.)

LUCAS. What?

WILLIE. *(Sudden, to EUGENE)* Take the painting. *(Eugene stops; looks at him.)* Take it.

(EUGENE picks up the painting. The others react.)

SYLVIA. Eugene, what on—sit down. Sit—My Kidman! You can't!

EUGENE. It's not yours, Mother.

(He heads for the door.)

SYLVIA. Eugene, stop it! Stop it, thief! Thief!

(But before anyone can move, he goes.
Blackout)

Scene 21

(Jenny's apartment. JENNY and CHARLIE are watching television. JENNY fools with the rabbit ears.)

JENNY. There ... there...

(She backs up.)

CHARLIE. Oh.
JENNY. I hate that.

(She gets close again.)

CHARLIE. There it is!
JENNY. Yeah, but I can't stand here all night.
CHARLIE. Try a different thing with the antenna. Like, get it so the pictures not really right, and then when you back up, maybe it'll clear out.
JENNY. Does that work?
CHARLIE. Yeah, it works. Mac used to do it all the time. Here, let me.

(He goes to work on the rabbit ears. She goes back to the table.)

JENNY. I think we're gonna have to break down and buy another TV, Charlie.
CHARLIE. No, this is fine.

(JENNY picks up a pile of envelopes off the table.)

JENNY. No, we should just do it. Willie keeps sending these checks. I should just cash one of them, buy the both of us a nice dinner, and get a decent television set.
CHARLIE. Cable?
JENNY. Yeah, cable. Why not, cable.
CHARLIE. Whoa, whoa whoa, got it.

(He backs away from the set. The two of them watch, entranced.)

JENNY. That's beautiful.
CHARLIE. Okay. You want to cash one of those things, that's up to you. I'm just sayin', in terms of entertainment, our needs are taken care of. Ain't that right, Swee'pea.

(He turns to the bird and notices Eugene, standing in the door.)

EUGENE. The door was open.
JENNY. *(Startled)* I know, I ... Come in.

(She turns the television off.)

EUGENE. I tried to call. Your phone is still unplugged.
JENNY. I know. I'm crazy.
EUGENE. No, it's totally understandable. I brought you this.

(He brings forward the painting.)

JENNY. Oh.

EUGENE. I'm sorry I couldn't do more.

CHARLIE. *(Seeing the painting, stopping)* Good lord, you found my duck.

JENNY. This is the duck?

CHARLIE. That's the duck!

JENNY. It's not a duck.

(Happy, she takes it to a chair and sets it on it, so they can all look at it.)

CHARLIE. What do you mean, that's not a duck. That is a duck.

EUGENE. It's abstract, it can be anything.

CHARLIE. People say that, but I don't know.

JENNY. It's not a duck. It's me.

EUGENE. It is?

JENNY. Yes, of course it's me. Mac wasn't painting abstracts, all those years. He was painting me.

CHARLIE. Oh. *(They look at it for a long moment.)* Well girl, you look like a damn duck.

JENNY. I do, don't I? I do.

*(They continue to look at the painting.
Fade out.)*

End of Play

TALKING HEADS 1 & 2
Alan Bennett

Six of these monologues by the inventive author of *Beyond the Fringe* and *The Madness of George III* were revived Off Broadway with a stellar cast that included Lynn Redgrave: *The Hand of God, A Lady of Letters* and *Bed Among the Lentils* on one night; *Her Big Chance, A Chip in the Sugar* and *Miss Fozzard Finds Her Feet* the next evening. Also in the two volumes: *A Cream Cracker Under the Settee, Soldiering On* and *The Outside Dog*. "Diamond-cut ... classics.... Mr. Bennett's work is too seldom seen on these shores."—*The New York Times*. "Each character has his or her own verbal music.... *Talking Heads* has brought great joy to this ... season."—*New York Daily News*. (#9935)

SECOND LADY
M. Kilburg Reedy

Originally seen Off Broadway starring Judith Ivey, this remarkable play has been applauded in theatres nationally and internationally. Ideal for an actress in her forties or fifties, *Second Lady* is a powerful 70-minute performance piece about a fictional political wife. She has mislaid her prepared remarks and must draw on personal experiences to fulfill a speaking engagement. Her recollections bring her face to face with the truth about her life and marriage. "A searing and soaring experience."—*Hollywood Reporter*. Published with *Astronaut* and *Fairytale Romance* in *Second Lady and Other Ladies*. (#20941)

For more Broadway and Off-Broadway hits, see
THE BASIC CATALOGUE OF PLAYS AND MUSICALS
online at www.samuelfrench.com

GOOD BOYS
Jane Martin

A fierce encounter between fathers, one black and one white, opens a deeply disturbing chapter in their lives. The men relive the school shooting in which their sons died, one a victim and the other the shooter. When racial issues threaten to derail all hope for understanding and forgiveness, the black father's other son pushes the confrontation to a dangerous and frightening climax. This topical drama by the author of *Keely and Du* and other contemporary hits premiered at the Guthrie Theater. "Galvanizing."—*St. Paul Pioneer.* "A terrifying, terrific piece of theatre that is as memorable as it is unsettling."—*Star Tribune.* (#9935)

THE ANASTASIA TRIALS
IN THE COURT OF WOMEN
Carolyn Gage

This farcical play-within-a-play is an excursion into a world of survivors and abusers. It opens as a feminist theatre group is about to put sisterhood to an iron test: each draws the role she will play on this evening from a hat. The performance that follows is the conspiracy trial of five women accused of denying Anastasia Romanov her identity. The audience votes to overrule or sustain each motion, creating a different play at every performance. "Farce, social history, debate play, agitprop, audience-participation melodrama, satire [that] makes the head reel!"—*San Diego Union-Tribune.* Wild."— *Washington Blade.* 9 f. (#3742)

For comedy and drama for all-male or all-female casts, see
THE BASIC CATALOGUE OF PLAYS AND MUSICALS
online at www.samuelfrench.com

BARBRA'S WEDDING
Daniel Stern

The Schiffs are the only non-celebrities in their Malibu neighborhood; in fact, their shabby house is next to Barbra Streisand's mansion. As the play opens, Jerry is in a frenzy over the media circus surrounding Barbra's 1998 wedding. An out-of-work actor with one small TV role on his résumé, he resents his obscurity—he wasn't even invited to the wedding! He rages against Streisand, Hollywood, the media, his wife and everything else. His wife tries to leave him—but Schwartzennegger's Humvee is blocking the driveway. This anti-show business comedy by a Hollywood insider is a hilarious send-up with a happy ending. "A ... play in the mold of Elaine May's comedies about people brought near to madness by the quirks of life."—*New York Post*. 1 m., 1 f. (#4901)

DIRTY BLONDE
Claudia Shear
Original score by Bob Stillman

A bawdy New York hit with dream roles, *Dirty Blonde* is "hands down the best new American play of the season....Take off your hats, boys, Mae West is back on Broadway ... in a compact Rolls Royce of a vehicle. This is no evening of mere impersonation.... *Dirty Blonde* is a multi-layered study of the nature of stardom ... [that] finds the enduring substance in the smoke and mirrors of one actress's stardom, allowing Mae West to shock and delight once again."—*The New York Times*. Vocal Score available. 2 m., 1 f. (#6929)